D1171898

*The New Town and County Hall Series*
*No. 5*

# THE NEW LOCAL GOVERNMENT SYSTEM

THE NEW TOWN AND COUNTY HALL SERIES

GENERAL EDITOR
## PETER G. RICHARDS
B.SC.(ECON), PH.D.

# THE NEW
# LOCAL GOVERNMENT
# SYSTEM

by

## PETER G. RICHARDS

*Reader in Politics,*
*University of Southampton*

*London*
GEORGE ALLEN & UNWIN LTD
RUSKIN HOUSE · MUSEUM STREET

FIRST PUBLISHED IN 1968

© *George Allen & Unwin Ltd, 1968*

*Cloth Edition*    04 352022 7
*Paper Edition*    04 352023 5

72-37 29 81

PRINTED IN GREAT BRITAIN
*in 10 on 11 pt Times Roman*
BY HAZELL WATSON & VINEY LTD
AYLESBURY, BUCKS

# PREFACE

*The New Local Government System* replaces *The English Local Government System* by the late J. H. Warren as the general introductory volume to the New Town and County Hall Series. Mr Warren's book, originally published in 1946, has undoubtedly been one of the most successful general descriptions of local government. Essentially it was a study of law and administration. However, a new introductory book is now required because the range of study in local government has widened. The political aspect is more important than it was twenty years ago, partly through the continuing growth of party activity on local councils and partly through the ever closer relationship between local and central administration. There is also a greater sociological content to the study of local government – witness the nature of much of the evidence collected by the Maud Committee. Further there is a fresh impetus to the concern with management in local government. The study of management techniques is basically an examination of administrative method, but the tendency to think in terms of 'management' rather than 'administration' is perhaps more than a change in fashion in the use of words because management does convey the idea of a continuous search for economies. So this book, granted the limitations imposed by its length, does try to bring together political, sociological and managerial approaches to its subject.

The title, *The New Local Government System*, has not been chosen solely to indicate the succession from Mr Warren's book. There is a prospect of major and imminent reforms in our methods of local administration. These will affect the structure of local authorities, their duties, their finances, the relationships between elected members and permanent officials and, probably, the relationships of both members and officers to the general public. Some of the changes will be national and specific and stem from legislation; others will come from changes in local conventional arrangements. The pages that follow give an outline of the existing system but they also lay stress on present difficulties and shortcomings and so foreshadow the changes that must soon come. Since the book looks forward to the future, some of the material is controversial. Naturally, I alone am responsible for the opinions expressed.

It is hoped that the book will be of use to several classes of reader.

Many people are prompted by a social conscience that urges them to learn more of public life and activity. Elected members of local councils may seek a fuller understanding of the system to which they contribute many hours of spare time. In particular, the book should assist young local government officers preparing for examinations by encouraging them to think and argue about their future role in society.

I am much indebted to Mr Frank Harris, Principal City Officer and Town Clerk, Newcastle-upon-Tyne, who supplied me with invaluable material about administrative reforms in that city. My best thanks are also due to Miss Jill Boyle, who typed the first drafts and to Miss D. Marshallsay, B.A., A.L.A., Librarian of the Ford Collection of Parliamentary Papers at my University who has prepared the index. My wife has undertaken her customary task of putting a final polish on the material sent to the printer.

PETER G. RICHARDS

University of Southampton
January 1968.

# CONTENTS

---

# Chapter 1

# INTRODUCTION THROUGH HISTORY

The present system of local government in England and Wales cannot be fully appreciated without reference to the past. Equally, the need for a new style in local government cannot be shown without a survey of the defects in the present system. Yet the history of local government is a vast subject on its own – witness the magnificent works of Sidney and Beatrice Webb. In an introductory book the historical element must be a mere sketch. This chapter is a sketch of the development of local government, but one that concentrates on the inter-relationship of local administrative areas, local services and local resources. It also tries to link the growth of local services with the dominant trends in political thought at least since 1834. How people react to social problems depends on what they feel to be morally right: the moral drive behind much of local government is one aspect too often overlooked.

## TRADITIONAL UNITS AND THEIR DECLINE

The three traditional units of local government in England and Wales have been the county, the parish and the borough. Each has had its own functions which were exercised with a large degree of independence, although the county justices had supervisory powers over parish officers. However, the sense of separateness was so strong that the idea of a *local government system* with major and minor local authorities with interlocking responsibilities did not emerge clearly until the latter part of the nineteenth century. By modern standards, the local units of government also suffered little central control. Central interference varied with the political situation of the time – the later Stuart Kings, in particular, tried to ensure that local positions of influence were held by their supporters – but local institutions were left to deal with local problems in the way they thought best. Since national grants were unknown until the eighteen-forties, the scale of county, parish and borough activity was minimal. Indeed, much effort was expended in the eighteenth century on the promotion of new local bodies to carry out tasks which the traditional authorities were unable or unwilling to undertake.

The county has its origins in feudal times when it was the territory granted by the King to an earl in return for acceptance of feudal obligations. After the feudal period justices of the peace chosen through the King's representative, the Lord Lieutenant, became responsible for county government. Initially the justices were essentially concerned with the maintenance of law and order. Thus their functions were primarily judicial. However, they had some administrative responsibilities, mainly for prisons and bridges, and they had to settle disputes arising out of the actions of parish officers. Visiting justices made irregular visits to parishes to inspect their poor law accounts.

Boroughs are based on charters granted at different times by the monarchy. These charters were valuable because they gave a small town the right to have its own justices and, therefore, to have its own court: this saved much difficulty and expense since disputes could be settled locally and without the need for a possibly unpleasant journey to the quarter sessions. Charters also gave the right to hold markets and so assisted trade and prosperity. They also provided for separate parliamentary representation, but this was commonly regarded as a mixed blessing because of the cost and danger of travel to Westminster. Often borough charters were granted by the King in the expectation of being able to control the nominations to the House of Commons made by the borough. The borough corporations themselves were usually renewed through a process of self-co-option.

The parish was originally the smallest unit of church organization. It gradually acquired non-ecclesiastical functions, starting with highways in the sixteenth century and the care of the poor in 1601. Frequently the word 'vestry' was used instead of parish because meetings to discuss parish business were held in the church vestry. The names 'open vestry' and 'closed vestry' described how far parish business was open to all parishioners; in a closed vestry decisions would be taken by the local elite – the people who were the largest ratepayers in the parish. Whether any particular vestry was open or closed generally depended on local convention rather than law.

For the common people the parish became the most important local unit of government as it had the greatest effect on their lives. The ancient liability that highways should be repaired 'by the inhabitants at large' was enforced through the parish. By the Statute of Highways, 1555, each parish had to appoint two surveyors responsible for the repair of roads in the parish, and the inhabitants were required to devote four days' labour to this work of maintenance.

The more wealthy members of the community chose to pay a highway rate instead of doing the work themselves and the money collected was used to pay the poor for working on the roads. The administrative duties of the parish became truly burdensome after 1601 when it was made responsible for the relief of the poor. The Elizabethan poor law required each parish to appoint an overseer who would impose a rate on the local inhabitants to raise money for the purchase of materials on which the poor could be put to work. The theory was that the goods made would be sold and the revenue could then be distributed to relieve poverty. Thus the poor would be helped, but they would also have to work to help themselves. The theory was commendable but, in practice, the idea could not work. The administration required was too complex for an unpaid parish officer to carry out: even when working materials were provided, paupers were often so old, ill or unskilled, or living in such bad conditions that useful work could not be done. The scheme collapsed and was replaced by the gratuitous distribution of relief financed by a parish rate. Especially in times of bad trade the cost of the poor law was heavy and often caused dispute within a parish.

Each parish carried out its duties through four types of unpaid officer – the overseer of the poor, the surveyor, the constable and the churchwarden. The duties of the first two have already been described. The constable was responsible for keeping the peace and took offenders before the magistrates. The churchwarden was responsible for the maintenance of the fabric of the parish church and, if necessary, collected a rate from the parish to pay for this to be done. Often the necessary funds were subscribed by the wealthy and church rates were rarely required. Necessarily they provoked opposition and indignation from nonconformists who did not attend the parish church. In 1837 the Braintree vestry refused to agree to a church rate and when the churchwarden tried to collect the money without authority his action was successfully challenged in the courts. In 1868 the Gladstone Liberal Government abolished church rates and cut another link between ecclesiastical and civil administration.

The parish officers were appointed at the vestry meeting. Since the work was substantial in amount and sometimes unpleasant, it was not always easy to find persons willing to serve. However, the system worked because of a general feeling that good citizens should accept a share of social responsibility. Often the jobs were passed round at the end of a year's duty. Some parishes had an understanding that a parish officer could nominate his successor. The overseer had the heaviest task and in some places a payment was made to him for his trouble; this might be done quite unofficially by means of private donations from the well-to-do inhabitants. Yet the whole system depended on part-time service and goodwill. It was quite unable to accept any wider responsibilities, so when demands came forward for extra and improved local administration the parish was by-passed. More efficient and more complex social provision required better qualified, paid and full-time staff which, in turn, required a larger unit of organization than the parish. Equally, the county and the borough were ill-placed to obtain extra duties, especially those involving the expenditure of public money. They were not representative bodies and not responsible to the public. So there were obvious grounds for refusing them any further taxing powers. In addition, some borough corporations and, indeed, some magistrates in urban areas were widely accused of corruption – of using official positions to secure personal gain. In the pre-railway age the larger counties were also regarded as too large a unit to be convenient for local administration.

Since the parish, the county and the borough were unsuitable to deal with the social problems arising from the growth of trade, the industrial revolution and the growth of population, new local government institutions were created. The three most important were the turnpike trusts, the Improvement Commissioners and the poor law unions.

The turnpikes were urgently needed to improve the state of the roads. In the eighteenth century there was a dramatic increase in the amount of road transport largely because of more trade but also because people started to travel more for pleasure or for health reasons. To place responsibility for maintaining roads on the parish was both inefficient and unfair. The largest parishes in terms of area were normally those in sparsely populated countryside, while the smaller parishes were in the more thickly populated districts. There was no correlation between the resources of a parish in terms of money or labour and the extent of its highway responsibilities: a parish with a tiny population could have a long stretch of a road running through it which linked major towns. Turnpike trusts were established by Acts of Parliament to charge tolls on travellers for using a road and the proceeds of the tolls could meet the cost of repairing the roads. Today many old toll houses can still be seen situated by the side of main roads.

The growth of towns aggravated many problems of urban living. As in the countryside there was a greater need to maintain roads, but there was also a need for drainage and for the effective maintenance of law and order, particularly the prevention of robbery. Many of the new industrial towns had no municipal corporation: elsewhere the corporations were in the hands of a limited clique and were not respected by the greater part of the citizens. So throughout the country bodies of Improvement Commissions were established by locally sponsored Acts of Parliament. The Commissioners were nominated in the local Act and renewed by co-option, but by the early days of the nineteenth century the principle of ratepayer election was introduced. Their powers varied and were defined in each local Act. In towns adjacent to rivers or the sea they often provided docking facilities and were known as Harbour and Improvement Commissioners. In general, they were responsible for lighting, paving and draining streets and for providing a watch – an embryonic police force.

Undoubtedly, the most expensive and most contentious branch of local administration was poor relief. During the eighteenth century the parish was already losing control of this function. Various Acts strengthened the power of the justices to supervise the distribution of relief. In 1795 the magistrates of Speenhamland drew up a scale of payments which related the amount of relief payable to the size of a pauper's family and to the price of bread; this Speenhamland scale was widely adopted by justices and overseers. Parliament also permitted parishes to work together in dealing with the poor. An Act of 1723 allowed parishes to join together and form unions which could build workhouses where the poor could live and work. This power was not widely used but another Act of 1782 authorised parishes to join together in unions so they could appoint paid officers to carry out the distribution of relief. These poor law unions were controlled by Guardians, originally appointed by the justices, but subsequently elected by ratepayers.

Two features dominated the law of local administration – it was both local and permissive. Only some main traffic routes were cared for by turnpikes; others were covered partially or not at all. Only some parishes agreed to join poor law unions. The powers of Improvement Commissioners varied as did their relationship, if any, with the local municipal corporation. Until late in the nineteenth century nothing existed that could be described as a coherent system of local services – instead there was a chaos of institutions, areas and rates.

## NINETEENTH-CENTURY REFORM

The political upheaval which produced the 1832 Reform Bill had an immediate impact on local administration. The first major change concerned the poor law. In 1832 a Poor Law Commission was appointed to report on the working of the existing arrangements and the Commission sent out investigators to examine conditions in about 300 parishes. These investigators may be considered as the forerunners of the present-day inspectorate. The Commission's Report portrayed a situation of confusion, incompetence and waste. The Poor Law Amendment Act, 1834, based on the Commission's recommendations, provided a new and uniform basis for poor relief. A central body in London, the Poor Law Commission, was to supervise the whole system – the start of central control over the detailed administration of local services. The central body united parishes into convenient areas for poor law purposes and in so doing ignored other traditional divisions. Thus many unions overlapped county boundaries. The poor law unions were also *ad hoc* bodies, i.e. they were formed to carry out a particular service. This was not a new idea in 1834 for turnpikes had then existed for many years, but the poor law unions were the first example of a pattern of *ad hoc* authorities covering the whole country; now there are many examples of this kind, River Boards, Hospital Boards and the area organisations of public corporations. The Poor Law Commission laid down strict rules covering the distribution of relief. The unions were to build workhouses and the distribution of relief other than to the inmates of the workhouse was banned: the regime in the workhouse was to be spartan to deter applications for admission. Local Boards of Guardians were elected by the ratepayers to run the workhouses, subject to national control.

The other major reform of the eighteen-thirties applied to the municipal corporations. Once more a Commission of enquiry was appointed and Assistant Commissioners were sent out to examine how the corporations were conducted. Again the report was damning. Some corporations were so decayed as to be virtually non-existent; many did nothing of value for the local inhabitants; some were corrupt. The Municipal Corporations Act, 1835, gave the boroughs a new constitution and insisted on proper financial management. Borough councillors were to be elected by the ratepayers and the House of Lords required that a quarter of the council should consist of aldermen elected by the councillors. All borough revenues were to be paid into a single fund to be used for the benefit of the inhabitants. The administration of justice was divorced from the administration of services and the borough justices were separated from the borough council. But in contrast to the Poor Law Amendment Act, the amount of central control was negligible. The major task of the borough was the maintenance of law and order and the 1835 Act decreed that a quarterly report from the local Watch Committee be submitted to the Home Secretary. A borough could also make byelaws for the good rule and government of its area which were subject to approval of the Privy Council. The Treasury was empowered to stop the sale and long leases of corporation-owned land. Yet the total effect of these controls was small. The 1835 Act did nothing to change the area of boroughs. It was applied to 178 towns. Other places which claimed borough status were ignored and the corporations deprived of recognition faded away. The City of London also managed to avoid coming under these provisions: many attempts in the following fifty years to reform London government were frustrated by the powerful financial interests of the City.

These two Acts demonstrate a remarkable difference of approach. The Poor Law reform was based on central control, uniformity, rationalisation of areas and the *ad hoc* principle. The Municipal Corporations Act emphasised the authority of local representatives subject to a minimum of central direction, maintained existing areas and created an organisation capable of dealing with a wide range of services. All these contrasts recur in the subsequent history of local government. Indeed, they form the basis of much of the current discussion about the shape of future local government reform.

In the eighteen-forties public attention was concentrated on the question of health. This concern was largely stimulated by Edwin Chadwick, Secretary of the Poor Law Commissioners, who was convinced that disease was the main cause of poverty and that the best way to help the poor was to remove the causes of sickness. Reports of official enquiries, heavily influenced by Chadwick, slowly created public willingness for government action. The two major reports on the Sanitary Condition of the Labouring Population (1842) and the State of Large Towns (1845) revealed almost unbelievable conditions of filth, squalor and a lack of drainage and pure water supplies. The Public Health Act, 1848, authorised the establishment of local Boards of Health to provide water supply and drainage, either where the inhabitants requested it or where the death rate exceeded 23 per 1,000. Municipal Corporations became the Boards of Health for their own areas. The work of the local Boards was to be supervised by a Central Board of Health. Earlier, in 1846, the Poor Law Guardians had been given limited powers to deal with insanitary nuisances in rural areas.

The public health legislation to a large extent followed the model of the Poor Law reform. However, there were differences, which grew larger as time passed. An element of central control was present and more *ad hoc* bodies were created. However, more scope was allowed for local initiative and the Central Board of Health never achieved the dominance of the Poor Law Commission. The Central Board was reorganised in 1854 and dissolved in 1858, its functions being divided between the Privy Council and the Home Office. (The original Poor Law Commission had been displaced in 1847 by a Minister, the President of the Poor Law Board, who was directly answerable to Parliament: but the central direction of poor relief remained firm.) The opposition to central direction on health questions was due to the disappearance of epidemics and the dislike of spending large sums of money that had to be raised by local taxation. Yet even when the *laissez-faire* reaction swept away the Central Board of Health in 1858 there remained 670 local Boards of Health which continued to promote more civilised conditions in urban areas.

After a decade of inaction at national level, the Royal Sanitary Commission was appointed in 1868. Its Report in 1871 set out the requirements 'of what is necessary for a civilised social life' which included a pure water-supply, sewage, burial arrangements and the inspection of food. A new government department, the Local Government Board, was created in 1871 to deal with these matters. In 1872 the whole country was divided up into urban and rural sanitary districts, the urban authorities being given wider powers. The urban authorities were boroughs, Improvement Commissioners and local Boards of Health: Poor Law Guardians became sanitary authorities for the parts of their union not included in the above. Thus while the Guardians combined both town and country for poor law purposes, they dealt with public health matters solely in the countryside. This separation of urban and rural areas was a reversal of one of the principles of the 1834 poor law reform and created the basis of the present distinction between urban and rural districts.

At this period the question of highway maintenance became acute as the turnpike trust system was breaking down. The new steam railways provided an alternative means of transport and adversely affected the revenues of the turnpikes, so reducing their ability to keep roads in good repair. There was also increased public opposition to the payment of tolls. In South Wales rioters destroyed turnpike gates. Consequently Parliament refused to renew the powers of the turnpike trusts when they elapsed and the disturnpiked roads reverted to the care of the parish. Even in the eighteenth century it had been widely accepted that the parish was not competent to maintain the roads and the obvious need was for the creation of a highway authority based on a larger unit than the parish. The county was unacceptable since the county justices were not elected. The alternative was to form unions of parishes on the model of the poor law. In 1862 the county justices were given powers to create such unions, but often these were based on the areas of the justices' petty sessional districts, not on the areas of the poor law unions. This added substantially to the confusion of local administration in rural areas. Highway districts were highly unpopular. They imposed a financial obligation upon the parish rate which had no connection with the extent of the traditional liability of the parish to maintain its own roads. Parishes suffered if small in area with substantial population; parishes gained if large in area with a small population. In some cases the gains and losses were heavy. Many large villages managed to opt out of a highway district by adopting the Public Health Act, 1848, and forming their own local Board of Health which entitled them to separate highway powers. In 1863 this trick was stopped by an Act which stipulated that only parishes with a population of at least 3,000 could adopt the Public Health Act. Meanwhile some of our present small urban districts owe their existence to the scramble to avoid inclusion in a highway union. The resistance to highway unions was so acute that in some areas they were never formed. In other places they were allowed to decay and responsibility for the roads again fell back on the parish. Elsewhere the areas were rationalised and made to conform with the poor law unions, yet this was often difficult because the poor law unions frequently overlapped county boundaries.

Today many local authority areas are anomalous; in the nineteenth century they were fantastic. Over a thousand parishes included one or more parcels of land completely detached from the main body of the parish; in the west of England the separated parts were occasionally situated in a different county. This jig-saw necessarily complicated local administration. The parish of Threapwood in the Wrexham poor law union was partly in Cheshire and partly in Denbighshire and so was part in England and part in Wales. A woman in the village, a pauper, went mad and had to be sent to an asylum. In England the charge for maintaining a pauper lunatic was 14s. a week, in Wales it was only 8s. a week. The question arose whether the woman was domiciled in the English or the Welsh sector of the village. The Clerk of the Wrexham Union discovered that the house where the woman was born was astride the county boundary. However, he was able to establish that the woman was born in the Welsh piece of the house and so saved his authority 6s. a week. This cameo is drawn from evidence presented to the Select Committee on Parish, Union and County Boundaries which reported in 1873. Gradually parish boundaries were rationalised but the process was slow.

Parish boundaries achieved greater importance because of both roads and education. In 1870 Gladstone's first Liberal Government imposed on the parish the responsibility of providing a school if an adequate one had not been provided by voluntary agencies – i.e. the churches. School attendance became compulsory in 1876 and free in 1891. The eccentric boundaries had effects which appeared inequitable. The main part of a parish could have a satisfactory church school but no provision for children in a detached piece some distance off; the whole parish was required to contribute to the provision of a school for the detached part. Even in 1870 the parish was obviously too small a unit to be a satisfactory education authority. However, since many parishes already had schools it was impossible to create school unions in which the cost could be pooled: such an arrangement would have aroused even more antagonism than the highway unions.

Over the years various pressures developed which made a democratic reform of county government long overdue. Agricultural labourers gained the parliamentary franchise through the third Reform Bill, 1884. The anomaly that boroughs, but not counties, enjoyed representative government had existed for half a century. The administrative duties of the county justice had grown steadily and so had the size of the county rate demand. In particular, the village constable was replaced by the county police force in 1856. It became clear that further services, notably highways, ought to be made a county responsibility in order to achieve better and more uniform standards of provision and to spread cost over a wider area. Finally, administration in the London area was seriously in need of reform. London had grown far beyond the area of the City, which had successfully avoided all attempts to modernise its constitution. Many important services were provided by the Metropolitan Board of Works established in 1855 which was based on a system of indirect election through a pattern of district boards. The Metropolitan Board had been responsible for substantial redevelopment in the West End but had become corrupt. Beyond question, London needed unified and democratic local government. These pressures, combined with the influence of Joseph Chamberlain and the Liberal Unionists within Lord Salisbury's Conservative Government, succeeded in making a major reform. The Local Government Act, 1888, is still the foundation of our present system of local government – outside London.

The Act had three major aspects. It created a new system of county councils elected on a ratepayer franchise: it defined the relationship between the county councils and the boroughs: it reorganised the financial relations between central and local government. When originally introduced the Bill had a further section covering the reform of smaller authorities within the county, but this had to be dropped for lack of parliamentary time. After a delay of six years this part of the reform was enacted in 1894.

The new county councils did not correspond entirely with the historic counties. Some were divided for administrative convenience because of the size of the county, e.g. Yorkshire, or its shape, e.g. Sussex. To a great extent these divisions often represented existing practice in that the county magistrates had met in separate centres and had levied separate rates. The bisection of Suffolk was based on acceptance of current arrangements. The problem of the metropolis was solved by carving a new county, the London County Council, out of Middlesex, Surrey and Kent, the L.C.C. boundaries being based on those of the superceded Metropolitan Board of Works. Two years after the Act was passed the Isle of Wight was also made a separate county. Thus the trisection of Yorkshire and Lincolnshire, the division of Cambridgeshire, Northamptonshire, Hampshire, Suffolk and Sussex, together with the new county of London created a total of 62 county councils out of the 52 geographical counties.

Initially the powers given to the counties were limited. Their major task was to care for those roads designated as county roads. A joint committee was formed with the county justices to supervise the county police force. They also inherited from the county justices an assortment of administrative duties, many relating to the issue of licences for various purposes. In subsequent years the counties acquired a wide range of functions. Indeed, the history of local government in the twentieth century can be largely summarised by listing the extensions to county responsibilities.

Much parliamentary time was consumed by the representatives of boroughs fighting for their independence from the new county councils. As originally drafted the Bill excluded only the very largest towns with a population of 150,000 from the aegis of the counties. This implied that all other boroughs would be subordinate to the county councils and would have to pay the county rate. Previously boroughs with their own quarter sessions had been exempt from the county rate because the administrative duties of the county justices had been carried out by their own borough bench. Under pressure from borough M.P.s the size of boroughs with county powers – i.e. county boroughs – was reduced to 50,000 population; four smaller boroughs, Burton-on-Trent, Canterbury, Chester and Worcester, were also admitted to the select band.

The financial sections of the 1888 Act were an attempt to secure some order and principle for methods of giving monetary aid to local authorities. At various dates since the Chadwick era Exchequer grants had been given in respect of education, police, highways, criminal prosecutions and some aspects of the poor law. The grants were designed to encourage better standards of provision in these fields and had grown steadily in amount. To place a limit on the cost of these grants to the national taxpayer, it was agreed that most of the specific grants mentioned above be replaced by a single combined grant, to be paid from a separate Local Taxation Account. This Account was to be supplied with 40 per cent of the product of certain national taxes – the so-called assigned revenues. The system did not endure because the proceeds of the assigned revenues did not rise as fast as the expenditure of local authorities and because successive Governments were unwilling to increase the range or percentage of the revenues paid to the Local Taxation Account. Although a failure, the assigned revenue idea is of much significance. It was an attempt to isolate central aid to local government from other types of national expenditure and thereby to reduce central supervision of local administration. It was also the start of a continuing argument about the relative desirability of general grants to local authorities as opposed to grants for specified purposes – a controversy examined more fully in Chapter IV.

As noted above, the reform of the small units of government in county areas was delayed until 1894. The urban and rural sanitary districts became urban and rural district councils as we know them today. In urban areas the change was little more than one of name. In rural areas the effect was more complex because the Local Government Act, 1894, provided that a rural district area should not overlap a county boundary. Since the rural sanitary areas were based on the poor law unions which ignored county divisions, some re-shaping of authorities was required. Rural districts acquired the duties of the rural sanitary districts, the highway responsibilities of the parish or those of the highway districts where such existed. The relationship with the Poor Law Guardians was reversed. Previously the powers of the rural sanitary district were exercised by those Guardians representing rural parishes: after 1894 the rural district councillors also served as members of the Board of Guardians. The parishes were also overhauled and given, like the districts, a rate-payer franchise. However, the powers of the parish had largely been transferred to larger authorities. Some parishes are too small to justify the creation of a council: the Act decreed that parishes with 300 inhabitants must have a council, those with less than 100 could not, and those between 100 and 300 could choose. In the absence of a parish council, parish business has to be transacted at a parish meeting. London was left untouched in 1894. This final remnant of eighteenth-century chaos was removed by the London Government

Act, 1899, which replaced a miscellany of district boards and parish authorities in the L.C.C. area by twenty-eight Metropolitan Borough Councils. These were thought of as a counter weight to the L.C.C. which the Conservative Government feared might become too powerful – a suspicion aggravated by what appeared to be its permanent Radical majority. Although the Metropolitan Boroughs were given responsibility for public health, housing, rating, libraries and recreational services, they never achieved parity of importance with the L.C.C. Due to the centralising tendency of modern times, as new duties were bestowed on local authorities they tended to go to the top-tier, the L.C.C.

Thus the nineteenth century witnessed a constitutional revolution in local government. The Public Bill steadily replaced the Private Bill as the main instrument of change. A reconstructed system of elected, multi-purpose authorities emerged; the *ad hoc* principle went out of fashion. Separate organisations each devoted to a particular function have advantages. They can have areas most suitable for their particular purpose; they can generate specialised enthusiasm; they are not distracted by other tasks. However, the drawbacks of *ad hoc* bodies are substantial. They create a complex jumble of administrative units that is highly confusing for the public; if they are representative, the result must be a multiplicity of elections; the necessary co-ordination between them is difficult or impossible to arrange; either they cover a wide area and become remote or they are too small to use skilled manpower economically. Since the later Victorians were keener than we are now to uphold the representative principle, the move towards multi-purpose local authorities was wholly logical.

The intellectual forces advocating reform were powerful but not homogeneous. Sometimes they came in conflict with each other; this is one reason why the pace of change varied. The interaction of these ideas provides some explanation for the pattern of events and requires some attention.

The eighteen-thirties and forties were dominated by utilitarianism, the creed spread by Jeremy Bentham and his disciple James Mill. They argued that human affairs should be so organised as to secure the greatest happiness of the greatest number, that institutions should be judged by their utility, i.e. by the extent to which they contributed to the sum of happiness. This is not the place to examine the philosophical and moral limitations of the utilitarian view: a study of local government must be concerned with its consequences. It was essentially a radical doctrine. It implied that existing arrangements and institutions should not be accepted unless they satisfied the test of utility. The chaos of local administration was so complete that patently it failed the test. But utilitarianism did not require a wide extension of the functions of the state. On the contrary Bentham tended to accept the principle of *laissez-faire* – that the government should leave things alone. State action was required only where it was necessary to increase the total of human happiness – if it produced more pleasure than pain. Today utilitarianism is out of fashion, partly because it is unsatisfactory in terms of ethics and partly because the measurement of pleasure and pain presents obvious difficulties. Nevertheless Bentham probably has a greater effect on contemporary thought and action than is commonly admitted. Of course, the concepts have evolved. Utility has been replaced by efficiency. Instead of a calculus of pleasure and pain, the modern calculus is of cost and benefit which can be measured, or estimated, at least in monetary terms.

Another influential concept was representative government. This idea has a long history. It had a great impact at the time of the English Civil War. In the eighteenth century the American colonists revolted over the principle 'no taxation without representation'. Any claim for representation raises immediate practical questions – who should be represented and how should their representation be organized? Throughout the nineteenth century an increasing number of public bodies were elected and the franchise was extended; in the early years voting was restricted to some ratepayers and the number of votes each enjoyed might vary from one to six depending on the rateable value of their property, but by the end of the period each ratepayer had one vote. So there was progress towards a ratepayer democracy. But those who urged the need for representative government were not necessarily favourable to democracy. It was widely accepted that those who contributed to the local rate should control the spending of the money raised. John Stuart Mill, the son of James Mill, argued convincingly that participation in the process of government was a valuable education in public affairs which helped to produce a sense of responsibility in the community and stimulated the creation of local leadership. Yet to give the vote to all implied that policy might be controlled by the wishes of uneducated people and of people who contributed little or nothing to the rates but derived benefit therefrom. However, the franchise for both parliamentary and local elections was steadily widened, partly because any limit appeared arbitrary and was awkward to defend politically, partly through the rise in educational standards and partly because limitation of the franchise caused administrative difficulties.

Utilitarian philosophy and demands for representative government reinforced each other in national politics. At local level they tended to come into conflict, at least before 1861. Chadwick regarded local self-government as potentially a vehicle for corruption. Utilitarianism demanded some element of central supervision of local administration to ensure that it was adequate and competent. The claim that the ratepayers, or their elected representatives, should decide how much to spend and how to spend it could easily clash with attempts to impose national standards. Controversy of this nature was widespread in connection with the development of drainage and other environmental health services. And the wider the representation, the greater the proportion of the populace to have the vote, the more likely were such clashes to arise: the poorer classes were more willing to take their chance of cholera and other diseases if this meant paying less in local rates. Opposition to central control led to the break up of the Central Board of Health in 1858. However, John Stuart Mill's *Representative Government* published in 1861 modified utilitarian doctrine in that it accepted the need to work with and through educated local opinion.

The third powerful force in local government was a feeling of humanity. This is an ageless sentiment; throughout time there has been some compassion for the poor, the ailing and the disabled. In a period when the Christian religion achieved great strength, one would expect humanity to influence public policy. However, it easily comes into conflict with other principles and baser motives. The administration of the poor law provides a clear example. Utilitarianism required a rigid, controlled and harsh regime to reduce cost, to stimulate self-help, in order to produce the greatest happiness for the greatest number. A humanitarian approach needed more flexibility, more charity and more expenditure. The reform of the poor law in 1834 was a triumph for utilitarian principles but slowly these were softened by slightly more generous administration.

Humanitarian thought stressed the dignity of the individual. It believed, to use a Victorian phrase, that people should be encouraged to better themselves. The argument can be presented with varying emphasis and degrees of sophistication. It is better for the country as a whole if everyone works hard to improve their position. God has given to each individual certain potentialities – it is therefore appropriate that these potentialities be used to the full. The same view can also be put without reference to God. Thus a climate of opinion was created favourable to state assistance to education, an attitude powerfully supported by the obvious need for a more highly skilled work force in an economy based on industrial processes of growing complexity.

Agreement that the state should take steps to promote human welfare necessarily required an erosion of support for *laissez-faire*. This doctrine, widely accepted in the early years of the century, argued that material prosperity was obtainable most speedily by fostering the spirit of free competition and leaving every man to work for his own interests. The role of the state, on this view, was minimal, limited to the preservation of internal order and security from external attack, and perhaps to provide bare essentials of life for those manifestly too weak to enter into the *mêlée* to aquire higher standards of comfort. But *laissez-faire* had no convincing solution to the problem of poverty caused through unemployment, to problems of public health or illiteracy. Even on questions of economic organisation it could not apply to the provision of services which required a heavy initial capital outlay and much interference with public and private rights. Free competition between railway companies, tramways, water and gas companies was obviously wasteful and undesirable. If price competition forced down standards of maintenance of equipment, the result was public danger. So the Victorians came to accept that there were natural monopolies that had to be controlled by the state, or provided by public authorities, to prevent exploitation of the consumer. Thus many towns provided their own water and gas supplies and later in the century electricity and tramways were added to the list of municipal trading services.

Support for representative institutions and humanitarian and utilitarian principles provided the driving force for change. But powerful pressures also worked against reform and hindered progress. Essentially these were the spirit of conservatism and the inevitable unpopularity of raising more money through taxation. These generalizations apply both to the nineteenth century and to our own time. It is easy to argue that things should be left as they are; that proposed changes are fraught with hidden difficulties; that the benefit of reform is exaggerated in relation to its cost. These attitudes will be promoted by wealthy persons and those in positions of authority who feel themselves threatened by change. Sometimes these established interests – Bentham called them sinister interests – have been so powerful as to be able to frustrate demands for reform: the history of the City of London in the nineteenth century is a paramount example of this situation.

## TWENTIETH-CENTURY DEVELOPMENT OF SERVICES

The present century has seen a vast growth in the scale of services provided by local authorities. This has been accompanied by an increase in financial aid from the national Exchequer and an increase in supervision by central departments over local administration. The structural changes have been less impressive, and have failed to keep pace with the development of functions.

It is possible to summarize the structural alterations fairly briefly. The two major *ad hoc* authorities, the School Boards and the Boards of Guardians, came to an end in 1902 and 1930 respectively, the greater part of their duties being transferred to county boroughs and county councils. A number of towns achieved county borough status before 1926 when the population qualification was raised to 75,000 and the obstacle to this promotion was made more difficult by changing it from Provisional Order procedure to a Private Bill: between 1926 and 1964 only one new county borough was created. As the larger towns expanded they quickly overspilled their boundaries; by agreement between the councils concerned there were a large number of adjustments to county borough boundaries which substantially increased their population, acreage and rateable value. A number of urban districts obtained borough charters and thus achieved added civic dignity, if only very few extra powers. The areas of urban and rural districts (but not the non-county boroughs) were also rationalized in the nineteen-thirties by the reviews carried out by county councils under the provisions of the Local Government Act, 1929. As a result of these county reviews the total of urban districts was reduced from 786 to 573 and that of rural districts from 650 to 477. The policy of the counties varied. Rutland and Radnor, the two smallest counties, were excused by the Minister of Health from making any review at all. Other small counties undertook reviews but left the number of district authorities unchanged – e.g. Huntingdonshire and Flintshire. In some large counties, like Devon and Somerset, the review was also notably ineffective. Elsewhere, as in Cumberland and Northumberland, the county pruned out the tiny urban authorities but left the rural councils virtually untouched. Other counties followed the reverse policy; Northamptonshire and Shropshire amalgamated rural districts and left the urban councils alone. Finally, some counties, e.g. East Sussex and Hampshire, took strong action in both urban and rural districts. The greatest concentration of small districts is in Wales. Essentially this is because the Welsh counties enforced a minimum amount of change, but in areas of sparse population it can be argued that lower population figures for rural districts are essential otherwise their areas will become inconveniently large.

While the total amount of change has not been inconsiderable, the constitutional framework established in 1888 and 1894 has remained basically unchanged. London is the exception. The London Government Act, 1963, pushed the metropolitan boundary out to embrace most of its suburbia and redefined the distribution of responsibilities between the upper- and lower-tier authorities. There has been almost continuous discussion since the last war of the need to redesign the local government system: the various schemes of reform and the barriers to change will be examined in Chapter VIII.

To revert to the growth of services: the first big move forward in this century came in the field of education. In 1900 the school leaving age was raised from twelve to fourteen. This created an immediate difficulty. The School Boards had been given powers solely to provide elementary education: if 'elementary' was defined as being limited to the basic skills of reading, writing and arithmetic, then children of ability aged twelve and thirteen would simply waste their time at the Board schools. Many of these schools started to provide more advanced instruction. In 1901 the Cockerton judgement held that the London School Board had no legal right to give advanced courses and provoked a crisis that demanded immediate action. The Education Act, 1902, abolished the 2,500 School Boards and transferred their responsibilities to the multi-purpose authorities. County councils and county boroughs were empowered to provide elementary and secondary education, but non-county boroughs with 10,000 population and urban districts with 20,000 population were made responsible for elementary education. Here is a principle that has not been widely used in local government – that the powers of an authority depend not only upon its status but also on its population. Since there was no arrangement for towns which subsequently achieved these population limits to acquire powers over elementary education, the result became anomalous; by the nineteen-thirties many boroughs and urban districts had grown rapidly and had no education powers although they were significantly larger than many authorities with these powers. The Education Act, 1944, concentrated education in the hands of counties and county boroughs, with the stipulation that limited powers should be delegated by county councils, especially to towns with a population above 60,000. Since 1944 the school leaving age has been raised to fifteen and there has been a truly enormous expansion of further and technical education. There has to be increasing co-operation between local education authorities over the organization of advanced courses in order to prevent wasteful duplication.

The abolition of the Poor Law Guardians was recommended in the 1909 Report of the Royal Commission on the Poor Law. The Report revealed wide disparities in poor law administration. Many of the Boards gave outdoor relief with varying generosity and provided medical services for those who could not fairly be described as paupers. This policy was defensible on both humanitarian and economic grounds: if the working population had medical attention and kept healthy, they were less likely to become a burden on the poor rate. The Royal Commission's Report was not unanimous because a Minority Report urged more drastic remedial action to remove the stigma of poverty and to break up poor law administration by dividing education and health aspects from the relief of poverty. The Liberal Government introduced old age pensions and compulsory health insurance and so eased the Guardians' task. Yet no action was taken to transfer the Guardians' duties to the major local authorities, perhaps because the Cabinet was immersed in many other violent controversies, perhaps because of reluctance to entrust the poor to county councils largely dominated by Tory landowners. It is also true, as was stressed by the Minority Report, that many Guardians had carried out their unpopular task with humanity and imagination. So the Guardians survived for twenty years more. In the nineteen-twenties more Unions were controlled by Labour majorities; these were accused by their opponents of extravagant expenditure. The Poplar Guardians led by George Lansbury at one stage refused to pay their share of the expenditure of the London County Council owing to the high cost of poor relief in Poplar. Allegations of corruption by the Guardians were widespread. An Act passed in 1926 gave the Minister of Health power to take over the duties of the Guardians if he found their administration to be defective; this was done in three places, Bedwellty, Chester-le-Street and West Ham. Ultimately the Guardians disappeared in 1930 under the terms of the Local Government Act passed the previous year. Their duties were taken over by the county councils and county boroughs and divided up between committees dealing with health, education and public assistance. The latter function was transferred to central government agencies in two stages with the establishment of the Unemployment Assistance Board in 1934 and the National Assistance Board in 1948. Also in 1948 came the final break up of the Poor Law when the Children Act and the National Assistance Act redefined the powers of counties and county boroughs to care for children, the aged and the infirm.

Personal health services remained in an administrative tangle until 1946. Hospitals had three origins – voluntary organizations, the Boards of Guardians and public health authorities. The Guardians were concerned with medical services for the poor while the health authorities were required to isolate persons suffering from infectious disease. After 1930 the medical wards of workhouses were taken over by the health committees of the counties and county boroughs and turned into general purpose hospitals. County boroughs, counties, and some other boroughs and urban districts were made responsible for maternity and child welfare from 1907 onwards and had opened clinics for this purpose. The National Health Service Act, 1946, transferred all hospitals to the new Regional Hospitals Boards but an expanded range of medical duties, including the after-care of hospital patients, the provision of health visitors and home helps was allocated to counties and county boroughs.

The construction of council houses and flats was started before the end of the nineteenth century. It was then thought of as an aspect of public health because the slums were breeding places for disease and their progressive replacement was a medical requirement. After the First World War the public provision of housing was accepted as a social need, and various Acts were passed which gave national financial assistance towards council building. Housing powers went to the boroughs, urban and rural district councils. This is the one modern service not allocated to county councils. Indeed, without the housing function it is difficult to see how many district councils could now justify their existence.

In the nineteen-twenties there was a great rise in the popularity of motoring. The increase in traffic created demands for higher standards of road maintenance. It will be remembered that highways were then the responsibility of the boroughs and districts, save that the counties maintained the more important 'county' roads. The Local Government Act, 1929, sought to improve the state of the roads in the countryside by transferring the powers of rural districts to the county councils. Towns with a population above 20,000 were allowed to 'claim' highway powers over county roads within their boundaries and all urban authorities remained responsible for minor roads. Rural districts and towns below 20,000 could also be given delegated powers over county roads, but this sort of delegation was never very important or satisfactory and has been steadily reduced. Care of roads demands highly skilled supervision and equipment which becomes more complex and expensive: here the case for centralization of responsibility is strong on economic and technical grounds.

Town and country planning is a further example of the transfer of functions to the higher tier of local authorities. All the earliest planning legislation from 1909 to 1932 had given boroughs and districts the opportunity to introduce local planning schemes. But this multiplicity of planning authorities proved a serious hindrance to the effective control of development; there were, for example, 133 planning authorities in the area served by London Transport. In fact, only a small part of the country had been covered by operative planning schemes prepared by borough and district councils, partly because of the intricate procedure and also due to fear of liability to pay compensation. The Town and Country Planning Act, 1947, centralized responsibility in the hands of counties and county boroughs and introduced a comprehensive system for the control of development. Again, there were also limited powers for counties to delegate decisions to non-county boroughs and district councils.

Fire brigades have also been transferred from second-tier authorities to county councils. Police forces of non-county boroughs have been absorbed into the county police. And centralization continues as county and county borough police have been amalgamated by Home Office Orders. Other powers have been taken away from local authorities altogether. This process started with the creation of Regional Traffic Commissioners in 1930 and the loss to them of the power to licence road passenger services. Relief of the unemployed went to the Unemployment Assistance Board in 1934. In the post-war period gas and electricity undertakings were nationalized and hospitals were taken over by regional boards. There seems no reason to believe that centralization has yet ended. Although local government now has a vast range of activities – these threaten to contain the seeds of decay.

On the other hand, present trends in political thought are still favourable to broader avenues for state activity. There is wide agreement that the duty of government is to promote the good life in a positive manner. It is not enough to clear up squalor because it may be injurious to health; eyesores must now be removed or prevented because they create a displeasing environment. It is not enough to give instruction in basic skills: education is now expanded to assist appreciation of all aspects of culture. Economic care is not restricted to the poor and the weak; economic planning is designed to advance the material welfare of all. So public administration is expected to do much more and a part of the additional tasks fall on local government. Fresh types of decisions may face local councils, e.g. whether to give financial aid to a local broadcasting service or whether to subsidize uneconomic passenger services. Recently they have obtained wider powers to develop civic amenities and promote industrial development. Even in a revised constitutional setting there can be new horizons for local authorities. In a period when ever more reliance is placed upon public administration, it would be strange if local government were allowed to wither.

---

# Chapter II

# THE BASIS OF THE PRESENT SYSTEM

The purpose of this chapter is simple yet fundamental. It is to anal-
yse the tasks undertaken by local government, the types of local
authority and the relationships between them.

### LOCAL SERVICES: THEIR PURPOSE AND EXTENT

Local authority services fall into four groups which can be termed
protective, communal, personal and trading. The paragraphs below
describe these functions in general terms. Their allocation between
the types of local authority is set out in detail in Appendix A.

The first group of services is designed to protect the individual
from a variety of dangers, e.g. fire, assault, robbery and epidemics.
Thus local authorities provide a fire brigade, a police force, a drainage system, refuse removal, food inspectors and weights and measures inspectors. These protective services constitute some of the
older branches of local administration, although rural areas lacked a
comprehensive fire service until 1938 as before then much reliance
was put on voluntary arrangements. Protective functions are nega-
tive in character as they promote good via the suppression of evil.
All are highly necessary but scarcely exciting. The licensing of
theatres, cinemas and of premises for music and dancing has a
dual purpose. It is a public safety measure and is also used to protect
public morals. A local authority can prohibit the public exhibition of
a film it judges to be offensive; this creates anomalies since licensing
authorities do not always take the same view about the same film.

Communal services again provide benefit for all, but in a more
positive way. In earlier centuries trade and travel were assisted by
parish responsibility for the roads. The towns repaired and lighted
the streets. Today the geographical distribution of population and
employment is guided by planning authorities, the beauty of the
countryside is protected and facilities are provided to assist its enjoy-
ment. Parks and sports grounds are also provided, particularly in
urban areas.

Personal services are of direct assistance to those individuals who need them. They form the most costly sector of local government functions. Education is the most expensive item. Other personal services include medical care and welfare services for children, the aged and the infirm. The use of these is optional. A parent need not send his children to a local authority school. An expectant mother need not attend the local maternity clinic. A frail old lady living on her own need not apply for a home help. But the percentage of people who decide not to make use of public services is declining. Most of them are free and are financed from the local rate fund supplemented by national grants. In a few cases a charge is made, e.g. home helps, but even then the charge may be wholly or partially remitted subject to a means test. Thus the personal services have an important equalizing effect on society in that they benefit the poor at the expense of the rich – or the richer; they benefit the sick and the family man at the expense of the healthy and the childless; they benefit those who use public services at the expense of those who do not although entitled to do so. Over the years the development of free services has been urged forward by left-wing opinion. There is now pressure for these benefits to be provided on a selective basis so they are paid for by people who can fairly afford them. Possibly local authorities in future will have to operate the means test principle more fully. Already it is widely applied to council house rents.

Trading services have declined due to the nationalization of gas and electricity. Municipal transport services may be taken over by regional authorities on which local councils will be represented. Water undertakings are slowly and somewhat painfully amalgamated and are now often operated by joint boards.

The division of local functions into these four groups is useful for the purposes of analysis, but the allocation of a particular service between the groups can be a matter of opinion. In a sense, all of them are communal. A sewerage system is both a protective service and a communal service. Education is provided for individuals, but it is a matter of communal benefit to have an educated society. And whether housing is regarded as a personal service or a trading undertaking must depend on how far council tenants pay an economic, i.e. unsubsidized, rent. Clearly, the sale of council houses is a trading activity. A few years ago it was arguable that town and country planning should be termed a protective service since it concentrated on stopping bad things, e.g. ribbon development; now it promotes environmental improvement and should be classed as a positive communal service. The introduction of tolls on new bridges is something of a reversion to the turnpikes and produces the flavour of a trading service.

Communal and personal services are those which show recent growth and these sectors offer wide and challenging opportunities for local government in the future.

It must also be noted that local authorities are not merely executive agencies. They exist not only to carry out duties but also to express opinions. This representative function has two forms. Local authorities can urge other public bodies to carry out policies which will be of local advantage. A Regional Planning Council can be asked to encourage industrial development in a particular area: Regional Traffic Commissioners can be asked to stop proposed fare increases on the buses. The second aspect of this representational activity is for one local authority to ask another, usually a larger authority, to do something. Counties receive many requests from county districts. The executive tasks of a parish are small, but a parish council may be very active in pressing local problems on the rural district or the county council.

### TYPES OF LOCAL AUTHORITY

The structure of local government in England and Wales can be illustrated by a simple diagram:

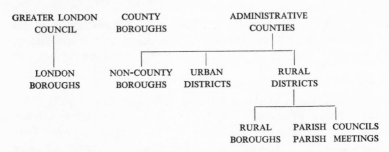

The left-hand side of the diagram describes the position in the metropolitan area; the right-hand side shows the structure in rural areas; in between come the towns in the provinces. In one sense the greatest distinction is between the county boroughs and the remainder of the country for these authorities alone provide the full range of local government services. Elsewhere, in London and in the counties, the services are divided between upper- and lower-tier authorities. In rural districts the parishes and rural boroughs form a third level of local government but, since their executive powers are so limited, here too there is virtually a two-tier system. The distribution of duties betweer upper- and lower-tier authorities is by no means uniform. The London Boroughs have a wider range of duties than county districts – this is an omnibus term covering non-county boroughs, urban and rural districts. As will be shown below, the larger county districts have wider responsibilities than smaller ones.

In the world of local government, size always tends to be measured in terms of population not of area. Appendix B shows the number of each type of local authority and the substantial variations in population within each category. Only the London Boroughs have any uniformity in size; this is because they were created as recently as 1963 and their boundaries were drawn, not to correspond with social units because it is difficult to discern any in London, but to obtain this relative equality. Appendix B shows that there are but six rural boroughs. This new type of authority initiated by the Local Government Act, 1958, consists of a non-county borough considered to be too small to carry out efficiently the normal duties of a second-tier authority. Under the 1958 Act county councils were to review the structure of their county districts and could, subject to ministerial consent, demote non-county boroughs to rural borough status. However, only a few counties had completed these reviews when the whole process was stopped by the appointment of the Royal Commission on Local Government to make a wholly fresh examination of local government structure. Meanwhile the six rural boroughs are a constitutional oddity; they have the powers of a parish but are entitled to the dignity of appointing a Mayor and a Town Clerk.

The county districts are housing authorities and provide the environmental public health services, e.g. sewerage, refuse collection and disposal and building regulation. They also provide parks and allotments. They are rating authorities although most of the money collected is passed on to county councils. Non-county boroughs and urban districts are responsible for the maintenance of minor roads; they may also repair the more important roads and pass the cost on to the county or – in the case of trunk roads – to the Ministry of Transport. The urban county districts may also run trading services, and the larger ones, roughly those with a population above 40,000, organize their own library services. In addition, a considerable amount of delegation of county council duties to the county districts has been arranged and this will be examined more fully below.

There is very little difference between the powers of an urban district and a non-county borough in spite of a marked contrast in their constitutional origins. Boroughs are created by the grant of a Royal Charter and some towns have acquired a collection of these Charters over the last 800 years. Urban districts owe their existence to parliamentary legislation. They may apply to the Privy Council for borough status, but such a petition is unlikely to succeed unless the urban district has a population of 20,000 and the goodwill of the county council. Privy Council decisions depend, of course, on ministerial advice. In recent years no new non-county boroughs have been created owing to the impending re-organization of the whole structure of local government. While the award of borough status gives added dignity to an urban district, this form of elevation is of trivial importance compared with promotion from non-county borough to county borough status which takes the borough outside the administrative county and gives a wide measure of functional independence and financial separation. Some boroughs are also known as cities: so also is the urban district of Ely. This title is commonly associated with ancient cities that were the seats of bishops. Today the honour is conferred by Letters Patent of the monarch, the last example being Southampton in 1964. But the award is of no practical value and gives no extra powers to the recipient.

County councils have acquired more powers steadily ever since 1888. They have no trading undertakings, otherwise they are concerned with all major local government services except housing and environmental health. County boroughs, as omnicompetent authorities, necessarily provide the full range of local services except a few which are rural in character, e.g. functions under the National Parks and Access to the Countryside Act. The reader is again reminded that the allocation of responsibilities between the types of local authority is set out in Appendix A.

The pattern of local government in London has always differed from that in the remainder of the country, and the position is now determined by the London Government Act, 1963. The new Greater London Council (G.L.C.) has amalgamated the former London County Council, Middlesex, the county boroughs of Croydon, East Ham and West Ham together with areas of the adjacent Home Counties which form part of the London conurbation. Within this area local government functions are divided between the G.L.C., thirty-two London Boroughs and the Common Council of the City of London. The G.L.C. took over services which demand large-scale organization and unified control, e.g. fire prevention, licensing of theatres, ambulances, and main drainage, while the Boroughs and the Common Council are responsible for personal and social services. Some tasks, notably housing, highways and planning, are shared between the two tiers of authority. The position about education is complex: in the inner area (the former L.C.C. area) the responsible body is a committee of the G.L.C., but outside the central zone the

Boroughs become the local education authorities. London differs also from the rest of the country in that some services that commonly fall within the sphere of local government are organized in other ways either by 'ad hoc' bodies, major examples are the Metropolitan Water Board and the London Transport Executive, or by the national government which ultimately controls the Metropolitan Police through the Home Secretary.

There is a large amount of co-operation between local authorities to achieve economies of scale and to prevent wasteful duplication of services. One council may use a service provided by another in return for payment – an arrangement very common in further education. Alternatively, councils may come together and form a joint committee or a joint board for a particular purpose. Services that are sometimes run on this basis include abattoirs, airports, passenger transport and water supply. The outstanding example of joint arrangements is now the police force: under the Police Act, 1964, many counties and county boroughs have been required by the Home Secretary to merge their forces in the interest of efficiency. Indeed, many of the new police authorities are really products of shotgun marriages, for the amalgamations were often sternly resisted by local opinion.

## COUNTY GOVERNMENT

It has been noted that the central contrast in our pattern of local government is between omnicompetence of county boroughs and the two- and three-tier arrangement in counties. London falls mid-way between these systems. County government provides the most complex network of institutions and therefore merits particular attention.

Counties do not permit easy generalization as they vary so greatly in area, population and economic and political characteristics. In size, Rutland presents a marked contrast to Devon. The population of Radnorshire is below 20,000, while eight counties are responsible for the well-being of over a million people. The word 'county' may stimulate a mind-picture of pleasant, food-producing countryside, but many industrial and mining areas are administered by county councils. The differences in size and social conditions necessarily have a great impact on the way in which counties carry out their duties.

County councillors are elected by the urban areas and parishes within the county in the same way as borough councillors are elected by the wards of the borough. Yet this is a similarity that conceals a difference. A ward, in most towns, is an artificial division created for electoral purposes, but a parish or a small town is more truly a social unit. Thus the *representative* responsibility of a county councillor may be more unique and personal than that of a borough councillor who is usually elected by a ward in company with two fellow councillors. The county councillor also has to travel away to the county capital to fulfil his duties and becomes something of an envoy to a higher authority; to a lesser extent the same is true of the parish representative on the local rural district council. All this should mean that county elections are more keenly fought than other elections because the winners have functions which are more vital and important than those who serve on other types of local authoritiy. In fact, county council elections are far more often unopposed than borough and urban district elections, although when there is an election the voting turnout is roughly the same in all kinds of authority at 40 per cent or a little higher. The explanation for lack of excitement about county elections is probably two fold: there is less party political activity in rural areas and because the county authority seems remote and distant there is less appreciation of the wide range of its activities. It still, however, remains true that the consultation of local opinion by county councillors can be a more complex activity than similar consultation in boroughs. Where a council is controlled by politics a councillor must pay attention to the views of his party colleagues and supporters. In rural areas where politics are less pervasive a county councillor will feel he should keep in touch with the attitudes of his parish council, rural district council or any other local associations within his constituency. There is much overlapping of membership between the layers of local government in the counties. Many county councillors serve on district councils; many rural district councillors serve on parish councils.

Because counties vary in size, there are also great variations in the number of second-tier authorities within each county. Nine have fewer than ten districts while Lancashire has above 100. In the smallest counties there could be a danger of the council being unduly dominated by the representatives of one or two large towns, but since the reorganization of boundaries in the East Midlands this is no longer a real possibility. Yet there is another problem of representation. If county councillors all feel a need to press the claim for their own 'constituencies', there will be a great amount of pressure on behalf of purely local interests. Very often the interests of a whole area, especially on planning matters, may differ from those of its separate pieces. Who, then, is to protect the county? In theory, the answer could be county aldermen: in practice, it is more likely to be county officials. The relative infrequency of county meetings, based on the tradition of quarterly gatherings, necessarily adds to the ability of officials to influence the conduct of business.

In the historical chapter it was noted that parishes often resisted being drawn into larger authorities, partly because they resented the loss of independence but perhaps even more because it was feared that any co-operation with neighbouring parishes would prove disadvantageous financially. Today the administrative county acts as a financial pool for the county districts within its boundaries. Counties spend far more money than districts but the latter have the task of levying the local rate. The counties impose a uniform rate on the districts – any variation will arise from use made of county services, e.g. some districts provide their own libraries. In consequence the more wealthy areas of the county tend to subsidize less well-to-do places. A prosperous town will make a greater contribution proportionately to county revenue than the ratio of its population to that of the whole of the county. This situation can generate hard feelings. It helps to explain why towns approaching 100,000 population have been eager to obtain county borough status and thus obtain financial independence. Conversely, the counties have had a strong motive for trying to block the ambitions of such towns. Every part of a county area will also wish to ensure that it is enjoying its fair share of county expenditure. Equally, the claims of a county councillor to secure benefits for his area must be judged in relation to the position of the authority as a whole.

When county councils were formed in 1888 it was widely assumed that they would exercise some supervision over district and parish authorities: this would have been a continuation of the tradition of surveillance by county justices. Counties do have some powers over the smaller authorities. They can change boundaries and electoral divisions of parishes, urban and rural districts. They also fix the day of elections within a week specified by law. That is why county district and parish elections are held on various days in contrast to the boroughs where the Home Secretary always chooses a Thursday. When a parish has a population between 100 and 300 the county may permit it to form a parish council. If a county decides that a rural district has failed to carry out adequately its housing responsibilities, the county may resolve to take over these duties itself, subject to a right of appeal by the rural district to the Minister of Housing and Local Government. In the case of non-county boroughs and urban districts, it is for the Minister to decide if any one of these authorities is defaulting on its housing duties and, if he does so decide, the function will then be transferred to the county council. Similarly, the Minister may decide that any district is failing in its public health responsibilities and transfer the duties to the parent county. Yet although these default powers represent a distant threat, they are not used. And the counties' constitutional powers over boundaries and elections are exercised after consultation with local opinion. There is no basis at all for believing that counties act as a strict father in relation to the work of their county districts. Counties do, of course, encourage joint action with smaller authorities, especially where this has obvious economic advantages; examples are the joint use of computers, organization and methods teams and the development of building consortia.

County-district relationships present acute problems. Resentment is caused by the fact that districts collect money for their county to spend. A further source of irritation, especially in the larger non-county boroughs, is the transfer of functions to county level. There have been varied attempts to alleviate such tensions by associating district councils with the administration of county services: the larger counties, in particular, have tried to overcome the feeling that they are remote and impersonal organizations. In a few cases, districts have been asked to nominate a representative on county committees. Alternatively, area sub-committees containing district representatives have been established to advise a county committee on the administration of a particular service in a sector of the county. Such local committees have been formed for education, highways, libraries and health service functions. They have not all been successful; some have faded away. Any organization with purely advisory functions will feel frustrated and useless when its advice is ignored. Since this type of area committee is essentially concerned to press for better standards of provision in its own part of the county, it is inevitable that much of its advice – or its claims – will be rejected on financial grounds. Another method of linking the two tiers of local authorities is to arrange for the larger county districts to exercise delegated powers over county functions: the practice of delegation creates quite special difficulties which are considered separately in the following section.

In contrast, the county boroughs are a simple form of institution. There is no parallel need to consult with its constituent parts. Jealousies between wards of a borough are relatively weak and easily smothered by party loyalty and organisation. The comparison of counties and county boroughs presents a paradox. On the one hand, there is less interest in county elections in the sense that county councillors are more often elected unopposed. The public also has less information and understanding of county government than it does of borough government. Yet the county appears to provide more oppor-

tunities for consultation – for example, the use made of county planning powers is widely discussed by county districts and parish councils. However, the paradox is more apparent than real. Activity at
election time depends rather on the level of party activity than the
level of public discussion. The greater complexity of the county's
institutional arrangements acts as a barrier to fuller general understanding, but it also provides extra opportunities for those who wish
to take an active interest in public affairs. Thus there is no necessary
contradiction in urging that the county form of local government is
more favourable to both apathy and public pressure than the all-
purpose single-tier authority.

Local government in the Greater London area occupies an intermediate position. The two-tier structure suggests a similarity with the
administrative counties. However, the distribution of functions between the tiers is quite different as the smaller authorities, the
London Boroughs, have charge of social services. If county government is described as top-heavy – then London government tends to
be bottom-heavy. The social effects of London's continuous urban
development in reducing local community sentiment and the intensity
of party political activity provide similarities with county boroughs
rather than counties.

## DELEGATION TO COUNTY DISTRICTS

Delegation by counties to their second-tier authorities is no new
arrangement. In their early years many counties used the districts as
their agents to help them to repair main roads. There is still a limited
amount of highway delegation to county districts but this is declining
as it is more efficient and economical for counties to care for roads
themselves. The case for delegation is that it brings local knowledge
and opinion to bear on the administration of county services; it is
obviously of little value in highway maintenance where the problems
are financial and technical. Delegation grew substantially in the post-
war period, chiefly through the provisions of the Education Act,
1944, and the Town and Country Planning Act, 1947. The Local
Government Act, 1958, added health and welfare to the list of dele-
gable services.

The growth of delegation has been due to a blend of political and
administrative convenience. When the administration of education
and town and country planning were reshaped the need for unified
responsibility, in the hands of county authorities, was accepted and
objections from the larger district councils to the loss of functions
were met with the compromise of delegation. The partnership that
delegation implies has permitted the joint use of the separate quali-

ties of larger and small authorities: backed by their financial resources, the counties undertake the overall planning of delegated
services, while detailed administration can be left to district councils,
which have a fuller knowledge of local conditions and are more
accessible to the general public. These advantages are considerable.
Counties are enabled to shed a great amount of routine while retaining ultimate control. County districts are allowed to participate in
services that otherwise would be beyond their scope. Delegation has
provided an element of flexibility by permitting the organization of
major services to be adjusted to suit local conditions. This flexibility
has had the further effect of reducing the urgency of a more general
re-organization of local government structure.

It is impossible to make many generalizations about delegation.
The legal position, the financial implications and the nature of the
co-ordination between district and county officials vary with each
case. But two basic conditions are observed. First, the county retains
the right to decide major questions of policy. Second, the county
retains control of expenditure falling on the county rate through the
approval of estimates submitted annually by district councils. An
agreement between a county and a district to share the administration of a function is embodied in a delegation scheme which is submitted for approval to the appropriate Minister. Any dispute over
the extent of delegated powers is settled by ministerial interpretation
of the scheme of delegation.

Education is the service in which delegation has aroused the
greatest controversy, for it provided the focus for arguments over
policy between counties and districts and was said to cause delays
and add to administrative costs. The Education Act, 1944, created
two types of body to exercise delegated powers – the divisional
executive and the excepted district. A divisional executive is a committee composed of representatives of the county council and a small
number of adjacent districts which takes decisions on matters of
current administration. An excepted district is a single authority.
Authorities with 60,000 population had the right to claim to be
an excepted district. A few slightly smaller authorities were also
awarded this status by the Minister of Education. Excepted districts
could draft their own scheme of delegation, after consultation with
the county authority, for presentation to the Minister for approval.
A divisional executive owes its existence to a scheme drafted by the
county council, and is, therefore, a child of county creation. An
immediate result is that excepted districts tend to have rather wider
powers, especially in the field of further education. The education
committee of an excepted district reports to a borough or district

council, and thus secures a popular mandate for its decisions that is not available to the divisional executive which can report only to the county. Further, the excepted district has greater cohesion since it is concerned with a single locality: a divisional executive may not achieve the same degree of unity of purpose. Finally, there is an important difference in the means of administration. A divisional executive carries out its duties through officials employed by the county council: an excepted district uses, in varying degrees, its own staff – officials of the local borough or district council – and the county estimates bear an agreed proportion of the salaries of those concerned. (Similar arrangements may exist for other delegated functions.) So the local Clerk, Treasurer, Engineer or Architect, together with members of their staffs, carry out much of the administrative work needed for the service of education in an excepted district. This gives a much greater sense of reality to the concept of delegation. The Education Officer in an excepted district is still an employee of the county council but he will spend the greater part of his time working with other officers of the local council and will come to be regarded as one of its chief officials. In sum, delegation to a powerful non-county borough creates a quite different atmosphere from delegation to an *ad hoc* body devoid of any kind of independent standing.

Delegation in educational administration has now been operating for a little over twenty years. There is no doubt that the second decade has been happier than the first. Far fewer disputes have occurred between partners to delegation agreements. The teething troubles are over and the delegation machinery, now well established, is made to work smoothly, partly because people learn to live with their frustrations. The circumstances of 1944, the demise of the old primary education authorities which caused much ill-feeling, have faded into history. Middlesex, the source of much trouble over delegation, has now been absorbed in the G.L.C. Finally, the domination by the Secretary of State over education developments entails a concentration of argument on educational issues between the central government and local education authorities rather than between counties and divisional executives.

The other major example of delegation is town and country planning: here counties have a variety of administrative arrangements. County districts with 60,000 population as 'excepted councils' are entitled to delegated powers and these may also be obtained by districts with slightly lower population in special circumstances if the Minister agrees that this should be done. Smaller districts may obtain (probably more restricted) delegated powers by agreement with the county council. Some counties also use area sub-committees to decide issues outside the range of delegated powers but which are not thought to be of sufficient importance to go before the county planning committee. Another difference is that some county districts exercising delegated powers employ their own planning staff, while others do not. In the larger counties various permutations of the above arrangements may exist side by side for different parts of the county area.

Of all local government services, the case for delegation is perhaps the strongest in town and country planning. This could still be true even were the structure of local government to be radically recast. A clear distinction can be drawn between the determination of the broad lines of future development and the detailed application of the plan. The former task requires an authority covering a wide area that can take a synoptic view of problems and overcome parochial pressure; the latter task demands detailed local knowledge and responsiveness to local opinion. Certainly local opinion should also be consulted in the formulation of long-term plans and this can be done more fruitfully if district or second-tier councils have experience of the detailed operation of development control.

Delegation of health and welfare powers requires less comment. The law governing the right to exercise these powers is the same as that for excepted districts for education. Delegation schemes for health and welfare functions are all similar because they follow a pattern laid down by the Ministry of Health. They have not all worked smoothly because of disputes over expenditure on staff and other resources. Authorities with these delegated powers are often areas with a rapidly expanding population and a high birth-rate – which makes them feel they need a higher standard of provision than the remainder of the county.

When a delegation scheme fails to work smoothly, it is not usually through defects in procedure. The root cause is more often a clash of interest between the parties concerned. A district will wish to attract as high as possible a share of county rateborne expenditure. Tension may be aggravated by clashes between personalities. If a county and a district are controlled by opposed political parties, friction can easily arise. Where a large non-county borough has been anxious to obtain county borough status, the county may have kept an over-jealous eye on the claims of the former to exercise authority and attract more powers. A watchful attitude by the county is also explained by the need to control expenditure and to achieve reasonable uniformity of standards throughout its area. Yet uniformity can be inimical to the purposes of delegation by frustrating local opinion. In circumstances such as these some conflict is inevitable: delegation merely provides a more complicated institutional framework in which negotiations can take place.

The total amount of delegation was reduced by the London Government Act, 1963, for there is now no delegation in the London area. However, the practice is still of importance for two reasons. It means that county districts with a population of 60,000 have a much bigger range of activities than smaller districts. Delegation also represents a truce between the claims of large authorities based on the size-efficiency equation and the claims of smaller authorities urging the need for consultation with local opinion. This democracy versus efficiency argument is the heart of controversies about the future structure of local government. Meanwhile, delegation remains a cumbersome compromise. It also involves elected members more deeply in the details of administration – quite contrary to Maud principles of management.

# Chapter III

# CENTRAL CONTROL OF LOCAL GOVERNMENT

To a large extent our system of local government has been a system of local *self* government. There is a strong tradition that local communities should be able to decide how to deal with their own problems. In the introductory historical chapter it was shown how the central guiding hand of Chadwick was deeply resented. Today central supervision has come to be accepted in general terms although complaints are still frequent about particular applications of it Clearly, if the national government did not have ultimate control over local councils the latter would tend to become autonomous units. No sovereign state would tolerate such a basic challenge to its authority unless it was prepared to become a federation of largely independent communities. At the other extreme, if local government were to have no ambit of decision not dominated by national government – then it would cease to be local *government* at all and become a mere agent of national government. So central-local relations demand a balance of control and independence, a balance of partnership and separation. The examination of why these relationships have evolved towards their present pattern is left until the final chapter. The immediate purpose is to describe the network of controls that surround local authorities.

One other preliminary note is essential. The orthodox treatment of central control divides it into three sectors, control by Parliament, Government Departments and the Courts. This fits the traditional tripartite division of political institutions into the legislature, the executive and the judiciary. However, if this model induces the idea that local government has three sets of controllers – Members of Parliament, civil servants and judges – then it is misleading. Civil servants advise Ministers how to use the powers made available to them by Act of Parliament. Members of Parliament are heavily influenced by party loyalty, so that the Commons normally accept the policy proposed by Ministers of the Government. Not all legislation is initiated by Ministers and the formal process of party discipline, the use of the whips, is not applied to Bills sponsored by backbenchers or by local authorities. But no Bill in either of these categories will pass if Ministers are deeply hostile to it. Thus both parliamentary and administrative controls over local government reflect the will of Ministers. Judicial control is a separate category; yet here again if Ministers dislike a judicial interpretation of local government law they could use their parliamentary majority to amend the law.

The threefold distinction between parliamentary, administrative and judicial control is retained in the pages that follow as it facilitates description. But it must not be forgotten that while civil servants, Members of Parliament and judges are not without influence, the essence of national supervision of local government is that it is undertaken on behalf of the Ministers of Her Majesty's Government.

### PARLIAMENTARY CONTROL

The legal basis of national control over local government is that local authorities have no powers other than those conferred on them by statute. Whether this statement is entirely true in relation to boroughs can be a matter for argument, but for practical purposes all local councils must be able to produce statutory authority for everything they do. If a council exceeds its powers, albeit unwittingly, its actions may be challenged in court where the principle of *ultra vires* will be invoked, and the extra-legal actions will be declared null and void. Thus local authorities largely carry out the administration of general principles of policy decided by the national legislature. Local authorities are not themselves legislative – i.e. rule-making – bodies except in relation to local bye-laws, and even here their decisions are subject to detailed government scrutiny and approval.

Local government law is complex, partly because it is highly detailed, partly because there are many varieties in the forms of legal power. Some statutory authority is contained in the Acts which established a particular type of local council. Thus the Greater London Council and the London Boroughs received powers from the London Government Act, 1963. More generally, however, powers are obtained from general Acts relating to a specific local authority function; obvious examples are the major statutes relating to public health, education and town and country planning. Most of the duties conferred on local authorities by Parliament are mandatory, i.e. compulsory, but in a few matters of secondary importance there is a choice of whether to use or 'adopt' powers. The Small Dwellings Acquisition Act, 1899, which enabled councils to provide mortgage loans to encourage home ownership, is an example of this optional arrangement. Another more recent case is the ability of rating authorities to decide under the terms of the Local Government Act, 1966, whether to levy rates on unoccupied properties. In 1963 Parliament gave local authorities a general optional power to spend a penny rate in any way for the benefit of its area provided that such activity was not subject to other statutory limitations. A third type of power is that conferred by a local Act, where Parliament has accepted a request by a local authority to give it additional authority. The procedure for obtaining such special powers is complicated and expensive; generally speaking, only the larger authorities seek to promote their own private Bills. A few pioneering ventures, notably the Birmingham Municipal Bank, have been started in this way, but many of the powers obtained from private Bills are relatively minor and raise no points of principle. Indeed, many private Bill powers could well be conferred on local authorities by general legislation.

Private Bill procedure, if widely used, could greatly widen the span of local government. Perhaps this is why Parliament has ensured that the promotion of a private Bill is a formidable obstacle race. A resolution to promote a Bill must be passed at two council meetings by a majority of the members present; public notices must be issued indicating the nature of the powers a council hopes to acquire; the Minister of Housing and Local Government may veto the promotion of a Bill. In boroughs and urban districts a town's meeting must be held to approve the Bill. (How many towns have a hall large enough to accommodate any significant proportion of the local inhabitants?) If the meeting approves the council's proposals, one hundred electors or one-twentieth of the electors, which ever is the less, can demand a poll. If the council's proposals are rejected, the council can demand a poll. This provides the only major opportunity in British government for the holding of a referendum. It is notable that referenda both here and in Australia and Switzerland, where they are more widely employed, tend to produce the result 'No'. However, if all these hurdles are surmounted, a private Bill goes before Parliament where, having been scrutinized by a body of Examiners to see it is in appropriate form, it then has to go through the usual routine of three readings in both Houses. Normally these readings are a formality. Discussion is usually restricted to the committee stage which is held before a small group of Members who sit in a quasi-judicial capacity hearing arguments in support of the Bill and any objections to it. Pleadings for and against a Bill are undertaken by members of the 'parliamentary bar', a special kind of barrister. The need to employ these parliamentary counsel adds greatly to the cost of the proceedings, especially if a Bill arouses objections and the committee stage is protracted. It was noted above that a Bill will not succeed if it incurs ministerial hostility; however, ministerial support is not an absolute guarantee of success, especially as the Bill has to satisfy the Lords as well as the Commons. The Conservative interest in Parliament has tended to be hostile to new extensions of local authority activity, notably in relation to municipal trading.

In addition to powers obtained directly from statutes, local government receives further powers from various types of Orders made by Ministers – Provisional Orders, Orders under the Statutory Orders (Special Procedure) Act, 1945, and normal Statutory Instruments. These are subject to varying degrees of parliamentary scrutiny. However, since they all engage the influence of Ministers, it is unusual for any parliamentary challenge to be successful. Many Orders of purely local application, e.g. compulsory purchase and clearance orders, asked for by local authorities, are approved or not approved by Ministers, and are not submitted to Parliament at all.

There remains the question how far local authorities can have non-statutory powers. The basis of the principle of *ultra vires* is that bodies created by statute can exercise only powers given to them by statute. Thus, the problem can affect only those authorities created by charter, not by statute – i.e. the boroughs other than London Boroughs. Ancient charters did confer powers on the municipal corporations but in modern conditions these have become meaningless or are of minor importance. The issue of the application of *ultra vires* to boroughs has arisen in a wider context because the Local Government Act, 1933, repealed certain provisions in the Municipal Corporations Act, 1882, relating to the expenditure of monies out of a borough fund; in particular there is now no specific requirement that these funds may be spent only on purposes authorized by statute. The judgement in *Attorney General v. Leicester Corporation* (1943) appears to show that boroughs are free from the restraints of *ultra vires*. But the legal position is very complicated, too involved to be discussed fully here. Suffice to say that Town Clerks discourage their councils from undertaking adventures on the basis of the Leicester case for two reasons. One is that it was decided in the Court of King's Bench, so that in any parallel case the Leicester verdict might be over-ruled in the Court of Appeal or the House of Lords. And even if boroughs do escape the *ultra vires* principle, they may not have complete freedom. A long-standing principle of the law is that 'a corporation may sue or be sued and do all acts as natural persons may'. This statement is not as permissive as it sounds since a natural person cannot impose a tax. Possibly, therefore, a borough cannot levy a rate to provide money for spending on a non-statutory purpose.

## ADMINISTRATIVE CONTROLS

The detailed supervision of the work of local authorities is undertaken by Government Departments. The extent of the direction varies greatly from function to function and between different parts of the same function. Central government is deeply involved in all major issues relating to education, police and town and country planning; it pays far less attention to the provision of public libraries, municipal entertainments and recreational facilities. The Ministry of Housing and Local Government is deeply concerned with the amount of local authority house-building and the standards of design and construction, but local authorities are wholly free to select tenants on whatever basis they think best. The Ministry of Transport is deeply concerned with major road improvements (trunk roads are entirely a Ministry responsibility) but leaves alone the maintenance of minor roads. This variation is due largely to the uneven amount of political interest attracted by local government functions and, inevitably, the more expensive services will induce greatest attention.

Most of the supervisory activity by the central government is authorised specifically by statute, but there are a few examples of Ministers being entrusted by Parliament with a broad oversight of a particular local government function. The Children Act, 1948, provides that local authorities shall carry out their duties under the Act 'under the general guidance' of the Home Secretary. The Education Act, 1944, is an even more extreme example of conferring wide power on a Minister by generalized wording. According to the Act it is the duty of the Secretary of State for Education, 'to secure the effective execution by local authorities, under his control and direction, of the national policy for providing a varied and comprehensive educational service in every area'. (In view of the current controversy about comprehensive education, it must be stressed that the word 'comprehensive' in the Education Act was used in the normal sense of all-embracing, not in the recent specialized sense which implies the abolition of selection for secondary education.) The language of the Act is strong and scarcely fits the conception that local authorities should govern: rather it implies that local education authorities are mere agents to carry out a Minister's will. This impression is supported by another section of the Act which authorizes the Secretary of State if satisfied that any local education authority

'. . . have acted or are proposing to act unreasonably' to give directions accordingly. In fact, these draconian powers are not used. Yet they remain in the background and must overshadow any major dispute between the Ministry and local education authorities.

The Education Act, 1944, is vague in another important sense. It speaks of the national policy for education without defining what the policy is to be. Presumably the policy is to be decided, and redefined from time to time, by the responsible Minister. Thus the wide powers of the 1944 Act entitle the Secretary of State for Education and Science to press forward a policy of ending selection for secondary education.

Many other Acts give Ministers a strong reserve power over local authorities. If a Minister is satisfied that a council has failed to perform a particular function adequately he may be empowered to issue an order to the council to instruct it to do certain things, or he may transfer powers from a district council to a county council or he may take over the powers himself. This default power was first incorporated in the Public Health Act, 1875, in respect of sewerage and water supply but was never actually used. Similar provisions are to be found *inter alia* in the Public Health Act, 1936, the Town and Country Planning Acts 1947 and 1962, the Civil Defence Act, 1948, and the Housing Act, 1957. These certainly give Ministers a big stick to brandish at recalcitrant local councils, but they are called into effect very rarely; the best known examples relate to civil defence at Coventry and St Pancras. There is no difference between the political parties in the matter of these broad statutory powers over local government: both Conservative and Labour Governments have inserted default clauses into local government legislation.

In the nineteen-forties it was the fashion for major Acts dealing with local government functions to require local authorities to prepare development plans for ministerial approval. The idea was to force councils to take a long-term look at local conditions and to get them to commit themselves in advance to a programme of improvement. The practical effect of these development schemes varied considerably. The plans for future school-building rapidly became out-of-date and were ignored. Plans under the National Health Service Act, 1946, once approved became obligatory on local authorities unless subsequently amended by ministerial sanction. Development plans drawn up under the Town and Country Planning Act, 1947, although repeatedly changed, are the basis of all town and country planning controls.

One of the oldest forms of central supervision is the use of inspection, first employed by Chadwick in 1834 to review the activities of the Boards of Guardians. Four local authority services are subject to regular inspection, police, fire, education and children. Since three of these services are the responsibility of the Home Office, it follows that only two Departments supervise through inspectors. There are two aspects to an inspector's duties. Primarily he has to ensure that local services are efficient and that standards are maintained: he also advises local authorities and his own Department on matters of technique and policy improvement. The term 'inspector' is also used, rather misleadingly, to describe officials who preside over local inquiries of various kinds. Their task is essentially to hear objections to proposals and report thereon to a Minister – this function will be considered below in the paragraphs on the appellate functions of Ministers.

The process of inspection is concerned not so much with council policy as with the way in which council servants perform their duties. There are other types of control over officials. The Minister of Health prescribes by regulations the qualifications and duties of medical officers of health. Various controls over the appointment and dismissal of local government officers are described below (p. 97) in the section describing the role of officials. The most exhaustive control over personnel is to be found in the police and fire services where the Home Secretary can make regulations governing appointment, dismissal, discipline, and conditions of service. In the case of fire brigades the supervision extends to methods of training and the provision of certain items of equipment. And a minor curiosity of local government law is that the salary of county clerks has to be approved by the Minister of Housing and Local Government.

Various actions of local authorities require ministerial approval. Development plans provide one example; another is any proposal for the compulsory purchase of land or property. Many Acts require a Minister to adjudicate in a conflict between a local authority and an individual, but some such disputes go to a court of law. Parliament has been careful to protect private rights against unjustifiable interference by local government, but no clear line can be drawn between the sort of issue that goes to a Minister and that which goes to a court. The policy imposed by Parliament has varied. Before 1930 appeals against closing orders – that a house is unfit for human habitation – were decided by the Ministry of Health: now they go before a county court judge. It is still a matter of doubt whether a county court judge is best suited to consider the technical issues that may arise in such disputes. A better solution might be to create a special tribunal to deal with these cases.

If an authority makes a clearance order to compulsorily acquire an area of sub-standard housing and other property for the purpose of redevelopment, any appeal goes to the Minister of Housing and Local Government. The Ministry will send an inspector to hold a local enquiry into objections and to hear any claims that certain properties in the area have been well maintained and are, therefore, eligible for additional compensation payments: the sort of evidence heard at this type of enquiry will not be dissimilar from that presented to a county court judge adjudicating on a closer order. Ministry inspectors hold other types of local enquiry, the most common are those arising out of refusals to agree to applications to develop land by building or extracting minerals. Other examples are enquiries into objections over the compulsory purchase of land by local authorities for housing, school-building, road-widening, etc., and disputes over footpaths. The inspector does not himself make the decision. His task is to listen to evidence presented by both sides to a dispute, normally to visit the site in question, and make a report with a recommendation to the appropriate Minister. The Minister is responsible for the final decision and in the vast majority of cases will uphold the inspector's opinion. Since 1958 the reports of inspectors have been published, unless considerations of national security are involved, so it is possible to see if the Minister has overruled his inspector.

Ministers also adjudicate in disputes between local authorities. Here there are no public enquiries; the councils concerned submit arguments to the Ministry and the issue is decided within the Department. If education authorities are in dispute over which of them is responsible for the education of a child, the matter is determined by the Secretary of State for Education. If a similar issue arises over a child taken into care, responsibility is allocated by the Home Secretary. If a county council disagrees with a county district over the interpretation of a delegation agreement, the matter is referred to the appropriate Ministry. These provisions are not of great importance but they remove the prospect of potentially expensive litigation between local authorities.

The remaining types of administration control are all related to finance. Each new category of local authority created since 1844 has had to have its accounts examined by a government appointed auditor – now known as District Auditor. Boroughs outside London are the only authorities to escape: they can choose between employing professional auditors, using District Audit or choosing auditors by election – the latter method is quaintly archaic and is rarely used. The District Auditor has wide powers. He has to be satisfied with the accuracy of the accounts and the legality and reasonableness of expenditure. If dissatisfied under any of these headings, he may surcharge those responsible for the amount concerned, be they officers or elected members. In the past the extent of the auditor's powers have aroused much controversy and the issues involved are discussed in the final chapter.

Since local authorities obtain much financial aid from central government it is inevitable that these grants should form another means of central control. The nature of the control depends partly on the grant system. Where a grant is made for expenditure on a specific service, the way in which that service is developed can be greatly influenced by a change in the amount of the grant or by a change in its conditions, i.e. a Minister may alter the rules governing the eligibility of local expenditure to earn grant aid. In 1958 the number of local government functions which had a separate grant was reduced; central financial aid to the local rate fund is now largely distributed in the form of general grants not linked to expenditure on specific services. However, the general grant can exert much influence over the policy of local councils: if the grant is unexpectedly generous, councils will spend more freely, but if the grant does not increase as much as they hoped then they will be encouraged to cut back on their estimates. There is also a reserve power, never yet used, which enables the Government to refuse payment of the general grant to a local authority if the Government is gravely dissatisfied with the way in which the authority has been carrying out its duties.

The third category of financial control arises from the requirement that a council must obtain ministerial approval before it raises a loan. When a local authority proposes to purchase or construct a capital asset which will be of benefit to the ratepayers in the future, the expenditure is normally financed by borrowing so that the cost of the asset can be spread over a number of years. Thus the need to obtain loan sanction is a powerful ministerial weapon. If approval for a loan is not obtained, a council cannot go forward with any scheme for capital expenditure unless it is prepared to meet the cost from current revenue. Originally, the requirement for loan sanction was imposed so that Ministers could ensure that local schemes were both reasonable in terms of local financial resources and were also technically sound. This provided a safeguard for small authorities with less well qualified staff and enabled them to benefit from the wider experience of Ministry officials. Another advantage is that the system may promote co-operation between local authorities in that approval for a scheme, e.g. for sewerage or water-supply, may be withheld on the ground that the service could be more economically organized in conjunction with a neighbouring council. Since 1939, however, the major purpose of this control has changed, for it has become a vital part of the general supervision which the Government exercises over the national economy. In war-time this was essential to secure the distribution of resources needed for the proper organisation of the war effort. In peace-time it is necessary since the Government now assumes responsibility for the overall well-being of the economy, which demands a healthy balance of payments and high levels of employment and productivity. To this end, the total of capital expenditure allowed to all public authorities is fixed each year, and local authorities receive a ration from the amount. Thus local authorities have to fit into a national economic plan, and the amount of capital resources they are permitted to consume in any period will depend upon Government policy.

Regular complaints are made by councils that they are prevented from undertaking capital expenditure they feel necessary – especially on school buildings. In a national economic crisis arising from balance of payments difficulties or other causes the Government may veto all capital schemes of a type it considers to be less essential, e.g. building swimming baths or council offices.

The wide scope of administrative control requires regular communications between local authorities and central departments. Applications from individual authorities are normally dealt with through correspondence. From their side the Ministries issue a large number of publications, many duplicated rather than printed, consisting of circulars, bulletins and handbooks of various types. The Ministry of Housing and Local Government issues bulletins of selected appeal decisions to show planning authorities how the planning policy of the Ministry is developing. Many of these departmental documents relate to technical and highly specialized matters, but the Circulars often deal with questions of general policy. The importance of Circulars has grown so considerably that they are commonly treated as an additional technique of central control, rather than simply as a means of communication. Their contents vary. A Circular may be informative, and merely state that a new regional office of the Ministry has been established. It may explain the contents of a Statutory Instrument or how a Minister proposes to use powers given to him by statute. It may offer advice and guidance, e.g. on how to deal with a particular type of planning application. The most important Circulars are those which require action, e.g. asking a council to review its house-building programme or to make plans to re-organize secondary schools on comprehensive lines. Necessarily the literary style of the Circulars tends to be a reflection of their content; those which merely provide information are flat, if not diffident, but those which demand action are more forceful.

A third means of communication is through personal contact. When a council has a serious problem it may send a small deputation of councillors and officials to London to put their point of view to civil servants or perhaps even a Minister. Civil servants also visit local authorities, but such visits are most often made by officials with specialized qualifications, e.g. engineers, surveyors and planners. Senior civil servants, the members of the administrative class who have the greatest influence on Ministry decisions, more rarely travel round local authorities. This is a possible ground of criticism. It is arguable that central control would be more flexible, that central departments would have a fuller understanding of local difficulties, if there were more personal intercourse between Whitehall and Town Hall and County Hall. Yet it is not certain that local authorities would welcome more visits from civil servants. They are, quite rightly, jealous of their independence and would resent anything that seemed to be a call from a new type of general inspector.

The total of administrative controls is very great. No doubt, a good case can be advanced for each item in the catalogue. The danger, of course, is that their cumulative impact can have a deadening effect on the whole of local government.

### JUDICIAL CONTROL

Before the second half of the nineteenth century, Government Departments had few personnel and resources. Administrative control of local government in the modern sense was unknown and impossible. County justices exercised somewhat erratic supervision over parish officers, but the justices themselves and the municipal corporations enjoyed a high degree of independence. The means of redress for a disgruntled citizen was to bring a legal action against a local authority. Thus judicial control formerly had an important effect on the development of local government. Today its effect is much reduced although certain legal principles inherited from the past still exert substantial influence.

A full discussion of the subject requires an extensive description of case law and the technicalities of legal procedure. This can be found in legal textbooks and will not be attempted here. However, a brief analysis of their legal position is necessary for a complete understanding of the constitutional position of local authorities.

Local government law can be divided into two sections. There are branches of general law, e.g. contract and tort, where special rules apply in relation to local government. A local authority cannot be held liable on an *ultra vires* contract because it had no power to make the contract in the first place. In general, a local authority is responsible for the tortious – i.e. wrongful – acts of its servants. Since an authority has no power to commit torts one might expect, following the doctrine applied to contracts, that it could not be liable for wrongs done by its employees. Fortunately, in this instance, the courts have not been logical or consistent. However, there are exceptions to public liability. If a local authority employee is acting under powers conferred on him personally by statute the authority is not liable for his actions. Local authorities also have a wide range of powers that are not possessed by a private person, rights of entry into private premises for certain purposes, rights to destroy infected goods or unsound food, etc. It follows that many things done by local government officers, which would be tortious acts if undertaken by private individuals, are legitimated by statute.

The other sector of local government law relates specifically to the way in which local authorities carry out their functions. Here again a twofold distinction can be made between provisions for appeals against council decisions and wider opportunities for ensuring that local authorities both keep within their powers and carry out their duties.

Magistrates' courts deal with disputes arising out of the application of building bye-laws and the naming of streets. County courts hear appeals against closing orders. The High Court hears appeals against compulsory purchase orders and clearance orders. This is a selection of examples, not an exhaustive list. But it must be noted that the powers of the High Court to review compulsory purchase and similar orders are very limited: any action must be started within six weeks of the order being confirmed and the Court can consider an appeal only on grounds of *ultra vires* or if it is satisfied that the applicant has been 'substantially prejudiced' by some defect in the procedure when the order was being prepared and considered. The time limit is necessary to prevent local authorities being required to restore houses that have been knocked down or to return land to its previous owners after work has started on the erection of new buildings.

The sector of judicial control which offers the greatest constitutional interest is that relating to the extent of local authority powers and the way in which they are used. The principle of *ultra vires* has been described above. Here it may be useful to give an illustration of how closely the principle is applied. In *Attorney-General v.*

*Fulham Corporation* (1921) the issue was whether Fulham Council had the power to run a municipal laundry. The Baths and Washhouses Acts, 1846–7, gave Fulham, as a public health authority, the right to provide baths and washhouses where people could wash themselves and wash clothes. The question was whether this power allowed Fulham to provide a service whereby the servants of the Council would wash clothes in return for payments to the Corporation. The Court's answer was 'No'. There have been many cases of this kind in which *ultra vires* has been used to obtain a ruling, often a restrictive ruling, on the meaning to be placed on words in local government statutes. Judicial proceedings can also be instituted to force a local authority to carry out its statutory obligations: such a case would now be a rarity, but in previous centuries there have been important instances relating to the maintenance of highways and the provision of drainage.

Local authorities can also be required to observe certain rules of equitable behaviour known as the principles of 'natural justice'. The two most important are that no man shall be judge in his own cause and that no man shall be condemned unheard. If an elected member participates in the making of a decision of benefit to himself, then it can be declared void by a court. In 1933 a decision of the Hendon Rural District Council to permit the construction of a roadhouse was quashed because one of the councillors present was financially interested in the project. There are difficulties and limitations connected with these declarations of interest which will be discussed in Chapter V. The other concept, that no man shall be condemned unheard, has led to the establishment of a wide range of public enquiries into the actions of public authorities, especially where these are likely to interfere with private property and other rights. It also governs the way in which these enquiries are conducted. The leading case here is *Errington v. Ministry of Health* (1935). The facts were that the Minister of Health had ordered a public enquiry into objections against a clearance order made by a local authority. The enquiry was duly held by a Ministry inspector, but subsequently the inspector visited the site accompanied by local authority officials but without the objectors. This was held to constitute listening to evidence from one side in the absence of the other, so the High Court quashed the Minister's decision to confirm the clearance order. It will be noted that this was not an action against a local authority, but an action against the way in which a Minister had used his supervisory powers over local government.

The outstanding example of judicial control in recent years is the three linked cases heard in September 1967 over the future of Enfield Grammar School. The dispute concerned the plan of the Borough Council to end selection for secondary education and to introduce comprehensive schools for children of a wide range of ability. For this purpose Enfield Grammar School was to be joined with a neighbouring secondary school and was to cater for the senior boys of the new institution. Objectors to this scheme contested it in the courts on a variety of grounds, some of which were rejected. However, the Court of Appeal decided that Enfield were proposing to act illegally, not because of the introduction of a 'comprehensive' syllabus, but because they were ceasing to maintain Enfield Grammar School as the age of entry to the School was being raised. The Council had a duty to maintain the School until it had issued certain notices and gone through the proper procedures for inviting objections, etc. In court the Council argued that the Department of Education had advised that such notices were unnecessary: this is an unusually stark instance of judicial control clashing with administrative control of local government. Immediately afterwards another action was brought against the Enfield Council based on the Grammar School's articles of government which required pupils to be selected on the basis of their previous educational records, the wishes of parents and the views of the headmaster. It was clear that the Council's comprehensive policy was incompatible with these articles of government and that the Council had ignored them. Once again, the Council lost the action. Immediately the Council asked the Secretary of State for Education and Science to amend the articles of government as he had power to do under the Education Acts. The Secretary of State thereupon intimated that he proposed to amend the rules covering selection of pupils at Enfield Grammar School by deleting the references to the candidates' educational record and the views of the headmaster, thus clearing the way for a 'comprehensive' entry. The Secretary of State announced he would allow three days in which objections could be lodged against his proposals. At an emergency session, held exceptionally on a Saturday, the High Court ruled that the time allowed for objections was unreasonably short and must be extended to a month.

The above paragraph is a scant summary of the Enfield saga. It does not describe all the issues for to do so would require a separate chapter. However, Enfield does show how the courts can insist that the law be respected and procedures for changing regulations be operated in a reasonable way even if – in terms of policy – the Minister gets his way in the end.

If there is disagreement over the meaning of words in a statute it is proper that the matter be settled in a court of law. To this extent, judicial control over local government is unavoidable. It remains, however, an unsatisfactory process. Local authorities are responsible to the local electorate and try to serve the public interest as they think best. They are in a quite different position to the ordinary defendant in that they rarely break the law deliberately. If they do break the law, it is normally because a law is unclear or becomes unclear when lawyers start arguing about it. Another aspect of litigation is the heavy expense, so local authorities are not challenged in the courts – other than before the magistrates – unless someone is prepared to spend a substantial sum. It follows that judicial control is partial in its operation. Some parts of local government law have been heavily contested in the courts while other parts go unchallenged. The statutes that are disputed tend to be those that affect property, i.e. rating, housing, compulsory purchase and town and country planning. The Enfield cases noticed above are untypical in the sense that the amount of recent litigation over educational administration has been small.

The merit of being able to appeal to a Minister rather than a judge is cheapness. Yet we recoil from the idea that a Minister should be able to interpret the law for this would place still more power in ministerial hands. There may also be a feeling that, as a dominant factor in the sphere of public administration, a Minister would be biassed in favour of local authorities against individuals, or would be guided by political considerations. A judge is held to be impartial and to give decisions based on recognized rules of statutory interpretation. However, since judges often find it possible to disagree, it is arguable that a judicial decision may be nothing more than the personal preference of a judge. Even so the personal view of a judge may still be preferable to the personal view of a Minister in that a judicial decision can be overruled by subsequent parliamentary discussion and action, whereas a ministerial decision is virtually irreversible in Parliament because of party loyalty and party discipline.

## THE ASSOCIATIONS OF LOCAL AUTHORITIES

It is convenient here to notice the associations of local authorities and the important functions they perform. Each type of local authority has its own national association which provides its members with a collective voice. These organizations are five in number: the County Councils Association, the Association of Municipal Corporations, which covers both county boroughs and non-county boroughs, the Urban District Councils Association, the Rural District Councils Association and the National Association of Parish Councils. There are also two similar bodies specifically concerned with education; the Association of Education Committees represents the local education authorities, and the National Association of Divisional Executives in Education has been formed by the authorities exercising education powers delegated by counties.

These national organizations have a variety of functions. They provide advice for individual local authorities. They give an opportunity to exchange opinions and experience about current problems. They provide representation on the wide variety of public bodies and advisory committees that are in some way connected with local government. The first four of the associations listed above nominate representatives to the various national joint councils which determine the salaries, wages and conditions of employment for all those on the payroll of local authorities. A list of the bodies on which the Association of Municipal Corporations is represented will be found in Appendix C: this list is worthy of study since it illustrates the complex net of relationships between local government and other institutions concerned in all manner of ways with public well-being. But the main task of the associations is to negotiate with each other and with government departments about proposals to change the law or any administrative practices concerning local government. Each of them is in touch with one or more M.P.s who may be asked, on appropriate occasions, to put forward in the House of Commons the point of view of a particular category of local authority. It is easy to overlook these activities and to underrate their significance, because much of the work is done in private and does not receive great publicity. In fact, government departments pay great heed to attitudes of local authority associations which often cause a Ministry to modify its policy. On questions related to reform in the structure of local government, Ministers have been notably reluctant to introduce any fresh legislation without first obtaining broad agreement from the associations.

The associations enjoy a large part of their influence through some self-denying ordinances. They avoid political controversy and operate on a non-party basis. (Perhaps this self-denial comes from the political parties in that they do not attempt to capture or control the associations.) The other inhibitions are that the associations evade issues which are not strictly local government matters and they also avoid becoming entangled in a dispute between any one local authority and a Ministry unless there are general principles involved of general concern.

# Chapter IV

# FINANCE

## THE SCALE OF OPERATIONS

Every benefit involves cost. Because local authorities organize a wide range of social provision, they consume a considerable fraction of the nation's resources of goods and manpower; in 1966, 789,000 persons were employed by local authorities. Or to put the matter in financial terms, local councils have an annual financial turnover of around £4,000,000,000. The spending and the collection of huge sums necessarily create a number of intricate problems.

A dominant feature of local finance is the meticulous care taken to control spending. Every authority prepares annually a detailed set of estimates to govern expenditure in the financial year starting on April 1st. Once approved by the council these estimates act as a check on subsequent expenditure. 'We cannot do anything about it this year because no provision has been made in the estimates', is a common explanation for failure to take action. Strict budgetary control is reinforced by auditing, by both internal and external auditors. Complicated rule systems have evolved to determine the legitimacy of expenditure. All this helps to prevent waste and corruption, although the auditing controls themselves cost a great deal of money.

The magnitude of operations is illustrated by the statistical returns of local expenditure and revenue for 1964–65, the latest year for which full information is available at the time of writing. In local finance a careful distinction is made between revenue expenditure and capital expenditure. Capital spending involves the purchase of an asset which will last for years to come. Thus money spent on school building or house building is of a capital nature while the money spent on the Clerk's salary is not. The distinction is important because local authorities can borrow to defray the cost of capital items. Not all capital spending is financed by borrowing; many small items are charged against current income. The relative importance of revenue and capital spending can be seen in the table below. Loans have to be repaid and the cost of loan repayment including interest charges is included in the figures of revenue expenditure; such costs constitute a high proportion of revenue expenditure on housing.

LOCAL GOVERNMENT EXPENDITURE
*England and Wales*
*1964–65*

| Service | Revenue Expenditure (£000s) | Capital Expenditure (£000s) |
|---|---|---|
| Education | 1,101,076 | 157,856 |
| Public libraries and museums | 32,022 | 5,044 |
| Individual health | 104,516 | 10,572 |
| Public health | 200,800 | 88,310 |
| Care of the aged, handicapped and homeless | 59,013 | 15,177 |
| Protection of children | 32,759 | 2,482 |
| Housing | 397,396 | 464,949 |
| Small dwellings acquisition | 37,961 | 262,467 |
| Town and country planning | 22,525 | 38,828 |
| Land drainage, river conservancy, coast protection and fisheries | 18,004 | 8,784 |
| Allotments and small holdings | 4,342 | 1,978 |
| Animal health, control of pests, etc. | 1,751 | 11 |
| Highways and bridges | 178,032 | 79,015 |
| Parking of vehicles | 5,621 | 5,962 |
| Private street works etc. | 12,262 | 4,793 |
| Public lighting | 23,730 | 6,441 |
| Fire service | 42,666 | 5,098 |
| Police | 176,050 | 13,823 |
| Administration of justice | 20,223 | 1,533 |
| Registration of electors | 2,871 | — |
| Council elections | 1,308 | — |
| Weights and measures | 2,477 | 98 |
| Registration of births, deaths and marriages | 2,681 | 13 |
| Civil defence | 8,883 | 1,014 |
| Miscellaneous including administrative expenses | 120,555 | 37,046 |
| TOTALS (£000s) | 2,609,524 | 1,211,294 |

*Source: Local Government Financial Statistics, England and Wales, 1964–65*

On the revenue account (p. 64) it will be noted that income from government grants exceeds that from rates. While this represents the national situation it conceals local variations, because the less prosperous areas enjoy higher rates of grant. The rate contribution to local expenditure will still be higher than the government contribution in places where rateable values are high. The figure for rents

LOCAL GOVERNMENT INCOME
*England and Wales*
*1964–65*

| Revenue account | £000s |
|---|---|
| Rents, fees, etc. | 525,036 |
| Grants: General | 790,217 |
| Specific | 311,464 |
| Rates | 991,159 |
| Trading profits | 3,850 |
| | £2,621,726 |
| *Capital account* | |
| Loans | 1,001,598 |
| Grants | 35,376 |
| Other sources | 174,320 |
| | £1,211,294 |

and fees is somewhat misleading in that it does not represent a net contribution to local income. Housing rents are more than offset by the cost of maintaining housing estates and the loan charges thereon. It will also be seen that trading profits make a very small addition to local revenue.

While the global sums involved in local finance are immense, the financial resources of individual councils vary greatly. This is simply illustrated by a few statistics showing rateable values of pairs of authorities of the same status.

| Type | Authority | Rateable Value |
|---|---|---|
| County councils | Lancashire | £78,000,000 |
| | Radnor | £521,000 |
| County boroughs | Birmingham | £50,000,000 |
| | Merthyr Tydfil | £1,300,000 |
| Non-county boroughs | Hove | £6,000,000 |
| | Montgomery | £15,000 |

The disparities are glaring and add much weight to the arguments about the overwhelming need for local government reform. Financial weakness is caused sometimes by local poverty and sometimes by the small area of an authority. In either case it is inevitable that local services will suffer unless heavy government subsidies are paid. Quite rightly, subsidies are paid to relieve poverty but not to relieve minute organization.

#### THE RATING SYSTEM

It was noted in Chapter I that the Elizabethan Poor Law laid the foundation for the present rating system. As local services developed their cost was met by extra rates added on to the parish poor rate: thus county rates and school board rates were linked with the poor rate. Such charges were imposed on the whole country, both town and rural areas. Urban areas had further expenses, mainly connected with sanitary services under the Public Health Acts, which were financed by a separate rate collected in boroughs and urban districts. In these areas two separate rates were imposed. Many towns obtained powers to unify the collection of money, but this wasteful and stupid duplication was not finally brought to an end until the passage of the Rating and Valuation Act, 1925. Since 1925 the boroughs and districts have been the sole rating authorities. Other authorities, the counties, the parishes and an assortment of joint boards with special powers, obtain income by precepting on the boroughs and districts. The level of the rate necessarily varies with the financial circumstances of each area. A county may not impose an equal precept on all its districts; some non-county boroughs and urban districts provide their own library service, so the expense of the county library service is charged only to those areas it covers. The amount of parish expenditure also varies, so the level of the rate in a rural district is not uniform but reflects the differences in parish precepts. Particularly in rural districts, and to a lesser extent in the urban county districts, by far the greater proportion of rate revenue is handed on to the county councils – because the counties are responsible for the most expensive services, especially education.

Liability to pay rates falls normally on the occupier of premises. Occupation is generally thought of in terms of control of the front door: a lodger does not control the front door and so is not liable. In some cases the owner of a property may be liable instead of the occupier(s). This applies to properties with a very low rateable value and to blocks of flats. Alternatively, an owner may come to an agreement with the rating authority to collect the rates from tenants along with the rents. For this trouble he receives a compounding allowance or discount from the rating authority. Until recently, occupation has also been defined as beneficial occupation: no rates were payable on empty premises. However, the Local Government Act, 1966, gives rating authorities the option of imposing rates on premises unoccupied for three months, or six months in the case of new houses and flats. Some property is excused from payment. Agricultural land has been exempt since 1929. Crown land is also exempt; in practice, the Treasury makes an equivalent contribution. Property used for or in connection with religious worship, public parks, sewers, lighthouses, buoys, beacons, sheds for housing invalid chairs, and the residences of ambassadors and their servants, are also exempt; and so are certain classes of machinery not deemed to be part of a building. Almshouses and other properties used for charitable purposes enjoy a 50 per cent reduction in the amount of rates payable, and rating authorities have a discretionary power to remit their rates altogether. This discretionary power to reduce or remit rates extends to other non-profit making institutions, e.g. social clubs and educational, literary and scientific bodies.

The Rating Act, 1966, was designed to ease the situation of ratepayers with low incomes. If authorized collection by instalments and provided for remission of rates for poorer persons not in receipt of national assistance. Each applicant for a rebate has to pay £7 10s of his annual rate bill; on the remainder a rebate of two-thirds is granted for a single person whose income does not exceed £8 a week, or £10 in the case of a married couple. These amounts are increased by 30s a week for each child. Where a ratepayer's income exceeds these limits, the rebate is reduced by 5s for every pound over the limit. The greater part of the cost of these concessions is met by a government grant. In fact, fewer people have applied for rebates than was initially anticipated. The heaviest pressure of claims arises in seaside towns where there are many elderly persons in receipt of fixed incomes often living in quite expensive properties.

How much is a ratepayer required to pay? This depends on two factors – the valuation placed on his property (the technical term is hereditament) and the poundage levied by the local rating authority. To give a simple example: if a house has a net assessment of £120 and the poundage charged is 10s in the pound, the liability for the year will be £60. It follows that the valuation of properties for rating purposes is a matter of financial concern to every ratepayer. The valuation is an attempt to define the annual value of a hereditament. While all rating valuation is based on this single principle, various means are used to arrive at the assessment in relation to different classes of property. However, shops and houses are assessed on the basis of a reasonable rent for the property; this figure is known as the Gross Annual Value. There is a standard scale of allowances to cover maintenance and insurance costs which are deducted from the Gross Value and this produces a second and lower figure, the Net Annual Value, on which rates are actually paid. Other techniques of assessment are used for factories, licensed premises and nationalized industries.

The task of valuation has been carried out by the Inland Revenue since 1948. Originally, of course, it was the duty of the overseer. Through the years various checks had to be imposed on the overseers to try to ensure that they did not undervalue property in their parish. There was substantial advantage to be gained from under-valuation in relation to charges assessed over a wider area than the parish, e.g. the district or county, because lower valuations allowed a parish to escape with paying a lower share of the total costs. The Rating and Valuation Act, 1925, abolished overseers and transferred the valuation function to county boroughs and area valuation com-mittees which covered a group of neighbouring county districts. Finally the system was nationalized in 1948 to achieve uniformity. As a new system of government grants was introduced at this time designed to give greatest aid to authorities with the lowest rateable values per head of population, this uniformity was essential to en-sure fairness in the distribution of the grant. In these circumstances, the inducement to undervalue property would have been very strong. The first valuation list produced on a national basis became effective in 1956. It showed conclusively that the earlier standards of assessment must have been extremely varied. To take the extreme examples: in 1956 the rateable value of Radnor was increased by 17 per cent, but nearby in Cardigan rateable value of the county went up by 160 per cent. Cardigan had been under assessed before while Radnor valuations had been very much higher. In theory, a completely new valuation list is produced every five years, but they tend to be postponed. The 1961 revaluation was put off until 1963; the 1968 valuation has already been put back to 1973. However, valuation of particular properties may be altered at any time to take account of extensions or improvements: by the Local Government Act, 1966, any such alterations and the assessments of new proper-ties are carried out on the basis of 1962 values to ensure that they are comparable with the original and unaltered items in the valua-tion list.

Any ratepayer may appeal against an assessment and argue his case before a local valuation court. A further appeal from a decision of this body can be made to the Lands Tribunal. To succeed an appeal must show that there is some injustice in the valuation. It is useless to go before the valuation court and say that you cannot afford to pay so much in rates! But if it can be shown that similar properties have a lower assessment, or that more desirable properties have the same assessment, or that the value of a property has been adversely affected by some local development, then an appeal can succeed.

In 1929, when agricultural land was derated altogether, industrial and freight-transport hereditaments were also relieved of three-quarters of their rate liability. This latter concession has now been withdrawn. Indeed, since the war the law on valuation for rating has been changed frequently in response to political and administrative pressures. For dwelling-houses built after 1918, the Local Government Act, 1948, introduced a new principle of valuation by reference to cost of construction, and for older dwelling-houses assessment was by reference to rents actually paid for comparable property in the locality in 1939. The Valuation for Rating Act, 1953, repealed the provisions about cost of construction before they had actually come into force, and valuation of all dwelling-houses was based on hypothetical rents in 1939 and certain other factors. The first post-war valuation list came into effect in 1956 and was based on these rules. Its impact on shops, offices and other commercial properties was considerable and Parliament passed another Act in 1957 to grant a temporary remission of one-fifth of the new assessments made on these classes of property. The Local Government Act, 1958, reduced the de-rating of industries and freight-transport hereditaments from 75 per cent to 50 per cent. Thus there have been constant shifts in the distribution of the rate burden between different categories of ratepayers. In the current valuation list, which came into force in 1963, the de-rating of industrial and freight-transport hereditaments was ended (Rating and Valuation Act, 1961). Dwelling-houses, shops and offices were rated also on current values, so there were drastic upward adjustments everywhere in the assessments of residential property. Of course, the rate paid by the residential occupier does not increase *pro rata* with the rise in assessments because the rise in total rateable values, including the greater amounts accruing from industrial premises, should permit broadly equivalent reductions in the level of the rate poundage. But any ratepayer will suffer if his own assessment has risen proportionately more than the average of assessments in his area. The rate burden also tends steadily to increase as local authorities are forced to pass on the rising charges for goods and services which they require. Yet the total *share* of rates paid by householders was virtually unchanged by the 1963 revaluation, although the position varied considerably in different parts of the country. Where the market value of residential property had climbed steeply there was a corresponding sharp increase in assessments, e.g. good-quality flats on the South Coast. In Bournemouth the residential share of total rateable value moved up from 48 per cent to 58 per cent; elsewhere, especially in industrial areas, the residential share actually fell. The 1961 Act empowered the Minister of Housing and Local Government to issue Orders which – subject to parliamentary approval – would authorize reductions in dwelling-house assessments in areas where householders were affected very adversely by the changes. The Minister decided, however, to make no such Orders because the changes in the incidence of the rate burden were not large enough to justify fresh impediments to a uniform valuation.

The rating of nationalized industries presents a special problem; their physical assets are not Crown property but are assessable to rates. Three of them, the railways, the gas industry and the electricity supply industry, have fixed plant obviously not self contained in any rating areas. Special arrangements operate under the Local Government Acts 1948 and 1958 for the ascertainment of the total rateable value of such assets in the areas of the owning Boards and the apportionment of the rate liabilities in respect of them among the rating authorities.

We now turn from valuation to the calculation of the rate poundage. The local financial year starts on April 1st, so in January and February estimates are prepared of spending in the coming financial year; these will be considered by the Finance Committee, possibly pruned back, and presented to the council for final approval. The detailed work is carried on by the Treasurer and his staff in consultation with the other spending committees. Obviously this involves pre-planning of future activities and requires important policy decisions to be made, so the preparation of estimates can be both a complex and controversial exercise. The final total of projected expenditure is a major feature of the local budget, but there are other factors which affect the extent of the demands made on ratepayers – national grants, local revenue from rents, fees and other charges and unspent balances, if any, from the previous year. A local authority is not entitled to accumulate surpluses on revenue account, so if expenditure in any one year is less than estimated the saving should be devoted to reducing the rate levy in the following year. Of course, an adequate working balance is permitted and a margin for unexpected contingencies.

When the figures for the various parts of the budget are available, the size of the gap between expenditure and non-rate revenue becomes apparent. This is the gap that has to be filled by local taxation. If the charge on the rate fund shows a steep rise on the previous year, there may well be demands for reductions in expenditure. The rate poundage is fixed by relating the income required from the rate to the rateable value of a local authority's domain; the latter is the sum of the net rateable values of all properties in the area. Thus if a council has a rateable value of £480,000 and requires to raise half this sum it would probably levy a rate of 10s 1d in the £ – the extra penny being required to cover the loss of revenue on empty property, various remissions and bad debts. This is, naturally, a greatly simplified picture of the local budgetary process; in reality, the calculations involved are highly complex. One other concept must be noticed, that of the penny rate product. This is the amount produced by imposing a rate of a penny in the £ and amounts to one two-hundred-and-fortieth of local rateable value, ignoring the effect of empty property. The penny rate product is a useful way of showing the cost of any new policy. To revert to the earlier example, an authority with a rateable value of £480,000 has a penny rate worth £2,000, so that a £10,000 scheme that earned no revenue of its own and attracted no national grant would cost a fivepenny rate.

Until 1967 all classes of ratepayers paid the same rate in the £. There have been, as was noted above, many shifts and adjustments in the methods of assessing various types of property, but at least the rate poundage was uniform. Now valuation is tolerably uniform but rate poundage varies because the domestic ratepayer is allowed to pay at a lower figure than other categories of ratepayer. This development is discussed more fully below.

### RATES – INADEQUATE AND UNFAIR?

Rates probably cause more irritation than any other form of taxation. Before examining the causes of this discontent, it is well to look at the few advantages that can be claimed for the system. The rating mechanism, in spite of complexities of detail, is traditional and is well understood. Now assessment has been nationalized, the valuations are generally just and, in any case, can be challenged by appeals. Since rates are payable on visible and immovable property, it is impossible to avoid paying. This means that the local authorities have a stable and reliable source of revenue. Rates are also a flexible tax in that it is easy to alter the level of the poundage. They are also economical to collect: according to the County Councils Association the collection cost is 1·2 per cent of the total revenue. Since rates are a tax on housing they act as a deterrent to under-occupation of property and may encourage people with excess accommodation to sub-let or move. And as the rates are imposed by local authorities they provide a degree of financial independence from the central government; without such independence, local councils would soon become mere agents of central departments spending from national funds. This last item in the catalogue is not an argument for rates *per se*, but it is an argument of basic importance for the retention by local authorities of an independent taxing capacity. So far no alternative to the rates has appeared to be politically or administratively acceptable; in these circumstances, the rates remain a bulwark of local autonomy.

Why then do rates provoke criticism? The first answer is psychological. Rates are a very obvious tax. Indirect taxes, for example those on tobacco, beer and petrol, are linked with the natural cost of the commodity: the public is generally aware that there is a substantial tax element in the total price, but the price is still accepted as the price *of the commodity*. Anyone entering a tobacconist's shop is not dominated by the thought that he is about to make a contribution to national revenue. Income tax, for the most part, is collected on a 'pay-as-you-earn' basis, so the wage and salary earner comes to accept the net amount of his weekly or monthly pay-slip as his true income. The tax and insurance deductions are accepted, no doubt regretted, but ignored when it comes to planning personal expenditure. You do not miss what you have never had. In contrast to P.A.Y.E. and indirect taxes, the rates are not hidden in any way. Money has to be extracted from disposable income and paid to the rates office. Since rate demands are usually sent twice a year, the sum involved on each occasion is substantial: however, authorities are now less unwilling to collect by more frequent instalments. Yet it still remains true that people are more conscious of paying rates than they are of most other forms of taxation.

There are many other objections. From the point of view of the local authority, the rates have an unsatisfactory tax base. Prices and costs rise ceaselessly; property values also rise but the quinquennial valuations are always postponed so that rateable values do not keep pace with the fall in the purchasing power of money. This means that rate poundages are forced up almost every year, thus creating annual discontent. It is also arguable that the reasonable rent basis of valuation for domestic property is largely spurious because, owing to the operation of rent restriction legislation, in many areas there is no free market in rented property. More equitable assessments might be achieved if capital values were used instead of hypothetical rental values. Householders may be deterred from expanding or improving their properties since to do so involves a bigger rate liability. There is also no connection between the use a ratepayer makes of local services and the extent of his rate bill. Whether this is a valid objection is a matter of opinion. Personal demands upon local services are either a matter of choice or need and, in so far as they result from need, the rate-supported services contribute to social equality. It is certain that areas in which the need for social welfare provision is greatest have the lowest rateable value per head and *vice versa* where needs are less rateable values are high. This creates a situation in which it is easiest to raise rate revenue where it is least required. High rateable values tend to produce low rate

poundages as illustrated by these examples for the financial year
1966–67.

| Local Authority | Rateable Value per head | Rate poundage |
|---|---|---|
| Bournemouth C.B. | £66 | 9s. 9d. |
| Oldham C.B. | £29 | 14s. 7d. |
| West Sussex C.C. | £54 | 7s. 4d. |
| Anglesey C.C. | £23 | 11s. 0d. |

The system of government grants is designed to assist the poorer
areas, but it is apparent that they do not entirely eliminate disparities.
(County rates in the above table are lower because, of course, they
do not cover the full range of local government expenditure and
have to be added to district and perhaps parish rates.)

All this makes up a powerful case against rates. Yet the main
criticism is that they fall unevenly on different classes of ratepayer.
Those who are liable to pay in relation to shop, commercial and
industrial premises can use their rate bill as an expense for which
an allowance is made in relation to income tax or surtax. No such
relief is available for the domestic ratepayer. Indeed, it is arguable
that to give income tax relief for rate liability would be unfair since
it would give no aid to those who need it most – those too poor to
pay income tax. The lower-income groups pay in rates a bigger
proportion of disposable income, i.e. what remains after deduction
of income tax and surtax, than the well-to-do section of the community. In 1963 there was a great outcry about the unfairness of
rating after the new valuation list had reassessed residential properties at current values. The storm of protest forced the Government
to appoint a committee to enquire into the impact of local rates on
households. This committee, under the chairmanship of Professor
Allen, issued its report in 1965 and demonstrated clearly the re-
gressive nature of local rates. Households with a disposable income
of £6 a week were shown to pay 8·2 per cent of it in rates; between
£6 and £10 a week the proportion fell to 6·2 per cent; at £30 a week
the proportion became 2·2 per cent. The rates, therefore, bear most
heavily on the poor. Their incidence is quite different to income tax.
A man with a large family enjoys substantial allowances in respect
of his children when income tax is computed. He also needs to
occupy more residential accommodation if he can afford it – and
this will make him liable to pay more rates. A lodger pays no rates
at all, at least directly. When the rating system was instituted on a
national scale in 1601 it was broadly fair as between individuals

since it was based on visible wealth, and the squire in the manor house could obviously afford to pay more than the tenant farmer or the yeoman. Today house occupation is a poor guide to wealth and ability to pay. This was conclusively proved by the detailed statistical information collected by the Allen Committee which emphasized that the greatest distress in paying rates was felt by elderly retired persons not in receipt of aid from national assistance, either because they did not claim when entitled to assistance or because their capital assets were so great as to disqualify them for relief. The Committee also showed that the 1963 increases in valuation had been sharpest on bungalows and flats in London and the South Coast; particularly on the South Coast this type of property tended to be occupied by retired people. Again the inequity of rates was demonstrated: the increase in rate demands after the 1963 revaluation had tended to be greatest where the occupiers were often the least able to bear the increased charge. Meanwhile, the rates rise steadily for everybody. In 1966 the average household paid £36 8s in rates, as compared with £18 13s ten years before. Thus rates nearly doubled in a decade.

Mr Crossman, Minister of Housing and Local Government from 1964 to 1966, was explicit in his hostility to rates. In the House of Commons on December 6, 1965, he said, 'Well, that is my view of rates: I am "agin" them, and that is why the two local government finance Bills that we are putting forward this Session should be regarded not as measures designed to make rating a good tax – that, of course, is quite impossible – but as interim devices designed to shore up this ancient monument which should not have been allowed to survive from the reign of Elizabeth I into that of Eliabeth II but which must now be prevented from collapsing altogether until we have had time to organize a planned operation for first demolishing rates and then replacing the system with a new local tax, fair, intelligible and capable of being administered reasonably efficiently.' The two Bills (now both Acts) the Minister referred to were the Rating Bill and the Local Government Bill, both of which became law in 1966. The Rating Bill, as noticed above, provided remission of rates for the poorest sections of the community subject to a means test. The Local Government Bill authorized that a lower rate poundage be charged to all domestic ratepayers. Thus the Rating Act is selective in its operation while the Local Government Act is not. According to the White Paper on Local Government Finance published in February 1966 (Cmnd. 2923) the aim of these new forms of domestic rate relief is to 'keep the average increase in rate poundages more nearly in line with the growth of the economy'. This will be achieved by steady increases in the amount of national grants. Clearly this will do something to mitigate the hardships of the rating system. But this policy has also a serious drawback. If rate income remains relatively static while costs and prices increase – local government will become more and more financially dependent on the national Exchequer. And, inevitably, he who pays the piper calls the tune.

Will the rating system remain if and when the whole structure of local government undergoes drastic change in the nineteen-seventies? Will future Ministers have the same reforming zeal as Mr Crossman? Can another more acceptable base be found for local taxation? A common response to this question is to suggest a local income tax. However, unless this were administered as part of the present Inland Revenue organization, the costs of collection would be prohibitive: in its present form the Inland Revenue system would be unsuitable since the collection is based on the geographical location of employers, not employees. Even were this snag to be overcome – there would still be formidable objections. Would it not be a mistake to add further to the disincentive effect of income tax? Would the Treasury be prepared to accept an invasion by local government into its key regulator of the national economy? Another popular suggestion is to alter the basis of rating, e.g. to rate site values. While this kind of adjustment might be an improvement, it does not really get to the heart of the problem. A satisfactory solution demands a new base for local taxation. Local taxation duties might be transferred to local authorities. But if the *level* of charge were to be fixed locally, then it would be cheaper to register vehicles in some places than others: it might well become economic to garage large lorry fleets in areas with lower duties. Yet if the level of tax is not a matter for local decision, councils have no control over their income. A sales tax is more obviously capable of local adjustment. The difficulty here is that people living in the countryside and in small towns spend money in bigger towns. To take the extreme case, London is almost a national shopping centre. So if the tax were collected by the present rating authorities on turnover in their own districts, rural areas would suffer badly. Were local government to be reorganized on a regional basis, this obstacle would partly disappear and some formula might be worked out to redistribute some of London's sales tax revenue to other parts of the county. But whatever the basis of local taxation, be it rates, vehicle duties or sales tax, it is impossible to avoid the situation in which it becomes easier to raise revenue in the more prosperous parts of the country.

## GOVERNMENT GRANTS

Many of the reasons why the national government has offered aid to local authorities have been implicit in the foregoing discussion on rates. As the state required local government to undertake new duties it usually made a grant in aid of the new service to ease the financial burden. Alternatively, grants were given to reduce the cost of an activity obviously of national as well as local benefit; a clear example is the grant made to meet the cost of criminal prosecutions in 1834. There is, of course, room for argument over which services are of national benefit. Drains are in the national interest because disease can spread. An efficient police force is of national benefit whereas a local playing field is not. Through the years views have changed on the nature and extent of the public interest and the term is now given a much wider definition than in the nineteenth century. The Victorian controversy about the exact distinction between what were described as local beneficial services and national onerous services deserving national aid now seems curiously antique. However, this distinction had an important role in the evolution of the grant system. Grants were also given to ease the burden of the poorer areas and to ensure that minimum standards were maintained over services thought to be of national importance. Financial recompense also has had to be made to local councils when the national government reduced their taxing powers, e.g. the derating of agricultural land and the partial derating of industry in 1929 and the domestic rate relief imposed by the Local Government Act, 1966.

There has been a succession of changes in government financial policy towards local authorities. Various types of grant have been used. The main distinction is between specific grants and general grants. The specific grant is given to aid a particular local service and is usually given on a percentage basis. An alternative is a unit basis – so much per house or flat. The percentage arrangement has two disadvantages. It may encourage extravagant spending, especially if the percentage grant is high: where a 50 per cent grant applies, the local authority can expect to recover half its expenditure. In consequence, central departments have to impose some check on local expenditure, probably by setting down categories of spending that will be accepted for grant purposes. This involves more central supervision of local government and an increase in administrative cost.

The general grant is a contribution to local rate funds not tied in this way. Again, it can take one of two main forms; either it can be designed specifically to help the poorest authorities or it can be given to all councils. Distribution is governed by a formula which will either try to assess the poverty of an area or will assess need by reference to the size and nature of the population. A general grant is simpler administratively. Arguably it is more conducive to local independence and freedom from central supervision. It also encourages good housekeeping by local authorities. The amount of grant is fixed before the start of a financial year (the normal practice is to fix it two years at a time) so the councils know in advance their income from the government. Any extra sums they may be tempted to spend fall squarely on the rates. Quite naturally, the general grants method has always been preferred by the Treasury. Essentially the history of the grant system over the past hundred years is one of continuous growth but also of ebb and flow between the general and specific categories. In 1888, 1929 and again in 1958 many specific grants were swept away and replaced by (more) general grants. The education grant disappeared in 1958. Critics claimed that its termination would lead to cuts in the standards of educational provision, but this did not happen because the increase in the general subvention was more than adequate to compensate for the termination of the separate education grant. The Labour Opposition was highly critical of the 1958 decision; however, when in office they did not reverse it. Indeed, speaking on the 1966 Local Government Bill in the House of Commons, Mr Crossman laid down two criteria for specific grants, that there must be a need to control the service centrally or that the expenditure involved must be distributed unevenly between authorities. The police are an example of the first category and coast protection of the second.

The main specific grants now in operation are for housing, police and roads. Road grants were restricted by the Local Government Act, 1966. Previously three levels of grant were paid on the more important thoroughfares, 75 per cent on Class I roads, 60 per cent on Class II roads and 50 per cent on Class III. Now 75 per cent will be paid of the upkeep of 'principal' roads, which correspond almost completely with the old Class I designation. The grant for school meals and milk was also removed. Yet the 1966 Act did introduce four new specific grants for the acquisition and development of land, the reclamation of derelict land, additional costs incurred from the presence of a substantial immigrant population and certain functions of port and airport health authorities. None of the sums involved are likely to be very large, but the new subventions will be of significant help to authorities particularly concerned with these problems.

General grants commenced their tortuous history with the assigned revenues of 1888, the failure of which was noted in the introductory chapter. During and after the First World War a variety of new grants was made available to assist particular services. Total national aid expanded from £23 million in 1915 to £76 million ten years later; the whole of this increase was in specific grants. The Conservative Government, with Winston Churchill as Chancellor of the Exchequer, decided to reorganize methods of central financial aid and as from 1929 all specific grants were replaced with a general grant, apart from those for education, police, housing, certain health functions and roads in county areas. The 1929 general grant was designed to compensate local authorities both for the loss of grants and for the loss of taxable capacity caused by derating of industry and agriculture. It was distributed on a complex formula which took account of the derating loss in each area and attempted to assess the degree of local need by reference to population, children under five years of age, rateable value per head of population, unemployment and population per road mileage. The compensation for derating was to be reduced over a fifteen-year period and finally eliminated while the local need element in the formula would be correspondingly increased.

Again the specific grants crept back with special help for the midwife service in 1936 and air-raid precautions in 1937. The post-war Labour Government favoured specific grants which were increased in range and amount. The 1929 general grant was replaced in 1948 by the Exchequer Equalisation Grant which gave aid solely to the poorer authorities. Local need was measured in terms of rateable value per head of weighted population. The figure for weighted population was obtained by adding to the actual population the number of children under fifteen and an additional weighting was added for country areas where the population per road mileage was less than seventy. This provided additional benefit for sparsely populated areas and those with a large child population. As compared with 1929, the level of unemployment was removed from the formula since local authorities were no longer responsible for public assistance. Grant was paid to counties and county boroughs on the basis of credited rateable value. This credited rateable value was the difference between local actual rateable value and what the local rateable value would have been had it been equal to the national average of rateable value per head of weighted population. The effect of this method was to bring the poorest areas up to the national average of prosperity. Authorities which equalled or exceeded the mean of affluence – as judged by this particular test – obtained no grant at all. For other authorities the state became a ratepayer to the extent of their credited rateable value.

This system lasted for ten years until in 1958 the Conservatives decided on another slaughter of specific grants, this time to include education. A new General Grant took their place again distributed on the basis of a formula. A basic sum was paid to counties and county boroughs on the basis of actual population plus population under 15 years of age. Additional grants were payable under seven headings; children under 5, old persons over 65, a high ratio of school pupils, high population density, sparse population, declining population and higher costs in the metropolitan area. The Exchequer Equalisation Grant to help poorer districts was continued in a slightly modified form and renamed the Rate Deficiency Grant. The amount of the General Grant has been fixed in advance at two-year intervals after complex negotiations with the local authority associations; the amount is not the same for successive years. According to the official rubric a number of factors are taken into consideration when fixing the total – the level of relevant local expenditure (this excludes expenditure on services which enjoy a specific grant), changes in local expenditure which lie beyond local control, the need to develop local services and the extent to which development can be afforded in the light of the national economic situation. Here is a clear recognition of the need to link the fortunes of local government with the general economic situation of the country.

The latest form of general grant is the Rate Support Grant initiated by the Local Government Act, 1966. This has three parts – the needs element, the resources element and the domestic element. The needs element is the successor to the General Grant of 1958: the resources element replaces the Rate Deficiency Grant: the domestic element is entirely new and is to cover the cost of reducing rate poundages for domestic ratepayers. There have been some changes in the formula governing the distribution of the general or needs element. New factors have been introduced relating to highways and school meals which have lost part or the whole of their specific grants. The needs element has been changed in that its amount is now fixed in advance; the superceded Rate Deficiency Grant was open-ended in the sense that if local authorities put up rate poundages the government had to pay more. This open-ended arrangement meant that the cost to the Exchequer could not be firmly estimated in advance and it may also have encouraged local extravagance.

The third leg of the tripod, the domestic element, cost £30 million in 1967–68 and £60 million in 1968–69 and produced a fivepenny rate reduction for householders in 1967–68 and tenpence off in 1968–69. It was planned to vote additional sums in later years but this was checked by cuts in government expenditure. The domestic element is

intended as a temporary palliative to minimize the hardship and unfairness due to the rating system until a more radical overhaul of
local finance can be undertaken. Meanwhile the total of the grant
escalates upwards. Supplementary amounts can be added after the
initial determination of the size of grant to compensate local authorities for rising costs and charges. The total rate support grant for
1967–68 was £1,283 million and for 1968–69, £1,395 million.

## CAPITAL BORROWING

Subject to Ministerial consent, local authorities may borrow money
to meet the cost of capital expenditure. The controlling department
is the Ministry of Housing and Local Government, except that the
Ministry of Transport is responsible for borrowing in connection
with local transport undertakings. Each loan has to be paid back
over a period of years, the length of the period depending on the
durability of the asset. The lifespan of capital assets is estimated on
a conservative basis for this purpose; for example, loans for baths
and washhouses must be repaid over 30 years, for houses over 60
years, for housing land over 80 years. It follows that at the end of
these periods the local authority will have a debt free asset; it may
achieve this position even earlier for no council is compelled to
borrow for the maximum permissible period.

Inevitably, this raises the question – is it a good policy to borrow
at all? An individual with an adequate income but no capital who
seeks to buy a house has no alternative: he must try to borrow by
raising a mortgage. But a local authority is not in the same situation.
It has a flexible source of revenue and can increase its income by
raising the rate poundage. Should ratepayers be forced to pay for
capital assets immediately, without recourse to borrowing? This
policy has one great advantage – cheapness. To raise a loan for a
period as long as 60 years is extremely expensive; the total cost of
borrowing £1,000 at 6 per cent interest over 60 years is no less than
£3,713. And today interest rates are often above 6 per cent, so there
is a case in terms of hard cash for paying for capital assets out of
revenue, and a few councils did so in relation to at least part of their
capital expenditure until the last war. Now the policy is out of
favour for at least three reasons. Durable assets will be of benefit to
the next generation of ratepayers, so why should the whole cost be
met by the ratepayers of today? This is a powerful argument which
is reinforced by the continuous tendency for the purchasing power
of the pound to decline. A pound borrowed now will buy much
more than it will when repaid in, say, fifty years time; admittedly
this is only a prediction but all economic experience suggests it is

a safe one! The faster the depreciation of currency, the greater the advantage to the debtor, the greater the loss to the creditor. The advantage to the debtor is offset by the interest that has to be paid but, unless interest rates are high, there is potential advantage in borrowing. At present interest rates are high, very high, and this encourages many authorities to charge small capital items to current revenue. To charge large capital sums to the rate fund would involve raising rate levels even more steeply and this would be politically unacceptable. If major capital schemes were financed from revenue, there is a danger that standards of provision would become not merely economical but parsimonious.

In local authority trading services it has long been a common practice to allocate any current surplus to a reserve fund which can be used to meet minor capital charges. Yet until 1953 councils had no general power to accumulate funds to meet capital costs: the Local Government (Miscellaneous Provisions) Act, 1953, does give such power, but it is hedged about with many restrictions. A capital fund established under this Act cannot be used in relation to trading undertakings or the education service. Contributions to the fund may come from the sale of property (provided that the property does not appertain to a trading service or to education), from any surplus in the rate fund and from a levy on the rate fund. Any such levy must be restricted to a fourpenny rate in county boroughs, a threepenny rate in county councils and a twopenny rate in county districts. The amount in the capital fund may not accumulate beyond the product of a shilling rate. Advances from the fund to purchase a capital asset or to accelerate repayment of existing debt have to be repaid by annual instalments. Interest may or may not be charged. It is important to note that this arrangement does not constitute borrowing; it is purchasing assets from accumulated balances. A clear distinction, therefore, must be drawn between this technique and borrowing from internal funds, e.g. superannuation funds, which is subject to ministerial loan sanction procedure. The 1953 Act provides a minor but useful avenue for capital financing. The limitations that surround it seem unduly strict and could well be reconsidered.

Ministerial control over local borrowing was firmly established by the end of the nineteenth century. Local authorities must apply for loan sanction and the Minister may hold a local enquiry to consider the application. Such enquiries are most often held when a scheme is unusual or controversial, or when compulsory acquisition is involved or when other public or private rights are involved. The reasons for control of borrowing have changed over the years. Originally, the concern was to ensure that local authorities were not

over-stepping the limits of their financial resources by incurring
unduly heavy commitments for the future repayment of debt. Such
Gladstonian prudence has now gone. The central government was
also concerned to ensure that engineering proposals by local authorities were technically sound: smaller authorities with inadequate
specialist advice have to be protected from the possibility of expensive mistakes. Now the main task is to ensure that capital spending
by local authorities is in conformity with the Government's overall
economic programme and, indeed, is in conformity with Ministers'
patterns of priorities. In any economic crisis, the order is likely to
come from Whitehall – no more town halls or swimming baths until
the national economic situation improves.

Once Ministerial permission to borrow has been obtained, a local
authority – and its Treasurer – are faced with two inter-related
problems, how to obtain the loan and whether it is preferable to
borrow on a short-term or long-term basis. The latter question involves attempting to forecast the future pattern of interest rates. If
they are expected to rise, it is better to arrange a long-term loan with
a fixed interest: if a fall is anticipated, it is better to arrange a short
period loan so that the money can be re-borrowed subsequently at a
lower interest charge.

Various techniques of raising capital are available to a local
authority. First must be mentioned the Public Works Loan Board,
established under an Act of 1875. The Board is financed by Government loans and the Treasury prescribes the interest rates to be
charged. In recent years there have been a number of shifts of
Government policy in relation to the P.W.L.B. Originally the idea
was that the Board should assist mainly the smaller authorities
which lacked both the prestige and experience to raise funds easily
in the money market. Then the post-war Labour Government decreed that all local borrowing, with some minor exceptions, should
be through the P.W.L.B. The theory behind this action appeared to
be that competition for capital by local authorities would force up
interest rates, and that higher charges might be at least partly
avoided by a single co-ordinated borrowing programme for central
and local government. In 1952 these restrictions were eased and
local authorities were encouraged to find their own sources of
capital. Some were reluctant to do so because the interest rates
charged by the Board were often more advantageous than could be
obtained elsewhere. So in 1955 the Government took firmer action
to cut down the use of these facilities. Three years later the Radcliffe
Report on the working of the monetary system urged that the
P.W.L.B. channel of finance be widened to limit the amount of

short-term borrowing by local authorities. This advice was not accepted immediately. However, an agreement between the Treasury and local authorities in 1963 provided that up to half of the capital requirements of a council could be arranged through the Board in return for an agreement by local authorities to restrict their temporary borrowing to 20 per cent of their total debt. This has not produced a great increase in the flow of funds through the Board; between 1961 and 1965 the indebtedness of local authorities to the Board was unchanged, although their total debt increased from £6,000 million to £8,400 million over the period.

Other techniques of borrowing can be described briefly. Subject to Treasury consent, local authorities can issue stock. Relatively large sums of money can be obtained by this means for a long period and these advantages are important to large authorities when interest rates are not too high. The most common methods are to issue mortgages or bonds. For technical reasons the bonds are simpler to administer and so are coming more into favour. Some capital is available from internal sources, e.g. superannuation funds. Short period and temporary loans are raised through the money market or from banks.

A general picture of local authority indebtedness can be obtained from the table below which shows how capital has been utilized and its sources:

ANALYSIS OF LOCAL AUTHORITY DEBT: 1967

| (a) by service | £000,000s | (b) by form of debt | £000,000s |
|---|---|---|---|
| Housing: sites, buildings | 4,390 | Stock | 658 |
| house loans | 677 | Mortgages | 2,102 |
| Education | 1,086 | Bonds and loans | 602 |
| Public Health | 422 | P.W.L.B. | 2,695 |
| Highways | 237 | Temporary loans | 1,256 |
| Trading Services | 324 | Internal advances | 357 |
| Other | 807 | Other | 273 |
| | 7,943 | | 7,943 |

*Source: IMTA Return of Outstanding Debt.*

Many authorities operate loan pools which simplify administration considerably. All borrowed capital and annual repayments are paid into a central loan account; the capital to be spent is also drawn from this account. As capital repayments are made on any one project, the money becomes available to be used on another scheme. Thus separate sinking funds are not needed and the total sums borrowed can be kept to a minimum. Until 1958 there was no general power to merge stock issues with other loans in a pool. Now the

Local Government Act, 1958, allows stock to be pooled by an authority with 60,000 population, provided it adheres to a model scheme prepared by the Ministry of Housing and Local Government and the Institute of Municipal Treasurers and Accountants; similar permission from the Ministry may be sought by smaller authorities.

What role should the Government play in relation to local borrowing? Two views on this issue emerge in the local authority world. There is a general desire to remain as independent as possible of central control. There is also a feeling that, as most local loans are required to carry through national programmes, the Government should facilitate borrowing and perhaps offer favourable interest rates. Some advantages would accrue from the establishment of a central organization to arrange a capital flow. The Institute of Municipal Treasurers and Accountants has urged the establishment of such an agency which would have power to borrow on its own account although it might be partly financed through the Consolidated Fund. This agency would not provide all loan capital required by local authorities which would continue to exercise initiative in fund raising. The scheme thus combines the attractions of local independence and central co-ordination. On the Government side there seems also to be two attitudes which ebb and flow. One stresses the need for a co-ordinated borrowing policy; the other wishes to avoid the strain on national borrowing facilities which would be imposed by an acceptance of full responsibility for local finance. There is no doubt that councils can tap funds from local sources that might not be available to the Government and most authorities at present manage without making use of the P.W.L.B. The problem is not lack of available capital, but high interest rates which are caused by national and international factors – not by the actions of local government.

# Chapter V

# THE CONSTITUTION OF A LOCAL AUTHORITY

A local authority, like any other piece of state mechanism, is governed by both law and practice. The conventions that develop within the formal structure of a local authority have a great effect on the way in which business is carried through and how decisions are made. No systematic description of the arrangements is possible since they vary between each authority. There is, however, one dominating factor – the extent to which a council is influenced by the political loyalties of elected members. The existence of political parties is unknown to constitutional law, but their importance in framing the conventions of public life can scarcely be exaggerated. The work of a local authority is based on the interrelationships of officials and elected representatives working together through a committee system. But, especially in the larger authorities, this pattern is substantially affected by party activity. To ignore the effect of politics on local government is unrealistic and misleading: a broad description of the political setting must be given before we move on to consider the respective roles of officers and councillors.

## THE IMPACT OF POLITICS

It is often argued that politics should have no place in local government. Certainly, there are some grounds for this view. Where elections are held on a party basis, no candidate other than those sponsored by a party has a real chance of success. Where one party is dominant in a particular ward or district, nomination by that party is tantamount to election to the local council, for electors become accustomed to voting on party lines and do not know, or do not care about, the qualities of the individual candidate. Attachment to a political party thus becomes an essential pre-condition of election to a local council; in so far as this limits the field of recruitment, the quality of elected members may be reduced. There must be many men and women of high ability, who would be willing to serve on local authorities, but who are unwilling to give unswerving support to a party or who happen to belong to a political minority in their own locality. The other main causes of complaint are that where councillors and aldermen organize themselves into political groups, decisions are taken by the majority group in private meetings, and that politics are allowed to affect details of local administration which are quite beyond the normal bounds of party controversy.

Equally, however, a strong case can be made in favour of party politics. Party activity does much to increase interest in local elections: party conflict tends to reduce the number of unopposed elections, and to raise the proportion of the electorate who vote in contested elections. Further, if a candidate is returned without a party label, it does not follow that he has no political affiliations but merely that he has not declared any he may have. To argue that politics should be taken out of local government is, in part, to misunderstand the nature of politics. In a democracy we argue freely about the proper aims and methods of public policy. This is political discussion. Inevitably, the major questions which confront local authorities, education, housing, planning, raise issues which are political in nature and attract the attention of political organizations. The idea that these matters should be left to 'the best man for the job' is fanciful since one cannot decide who is best man unless the opinions of candidates are revealed. The charge that party groups should not have private 'caucus' meetings to settle policy is countered by showing that this is analogous to what happens in our national government; no one suggests it is wrong for Conservative and Labour M.P.s to hold separate private gatherings or that party leaders should not meet in conditions of secrecy at Cabinet or 'Shadow' Cabinet meetings. Party organization in a democracy is essential for opinions to be organized into broad streams. The group or party representing the dominant stream of opinion becomes responsible for the conduct of public affairs for a limited time, and may be displaced from power at a subsequent election if it displeases the voters. It follows that where the business of a local authority is conducted on a party basis, the policy of the authority is more likely to be planned and consistent than if it depends on unorganized and changing views of individual councillors.

Whatever view one takes of these theoretical considerations, it is vital to recognize that the impact of politics on local government is growing steadily. Except in rural areas, most local elections are now fought on a party basis. What does vary, however, and what is most difficult to determine, is how far party organization affects the actual working of a local council. The variety of local arrangements is best illustrated by the description of extremes. In some councils, party loyalty matters little; members are elected on a party basis but, once elected, tend to act as individuals; committee chairmen and aldermen are chosen irrespective of politics and no group meetings are held. This is often the pattern in small towns and in non-industrial areas. At the other extreme, party governs everything important. The majority group meets to determine policy on major issues; it secures a majority on all committees; it nominates the chairmen and vice-chairmen of all committees; either it dominates the aldermanic seats completely or, more likely, by agreement between parties, the aldermen are shared in proportion to the number of their councillors; the parties require complete obedience from their members, and any councillor who refuses to support a party decision is expelled from the group and will not get party support at the next election. Such extensive party influence is common in large towns and other authorities dominated by the Labour Party. There are, of course, many authorities which fall in between the patterns defined above, where groups meet irregularly or committee chairmanships are not always distributed on a party basis. And sometimes where party loyalties are strong, the effect of politics is restricted because no group has an overall majority of seats.

Against this background of an uneven degree of party activity, the work of elected members, officers and committees continues. Where the party element is strong the ability of elected members to speak their minds freely in public is curtailed. On major issues the only free discussion takes place in the privacy of the party meeting where party policy is decided, if necessary by a vote. An elected member who finds himself in a minority among party colleagues is required to bow to the necessity of political unity and vote against his opinion at committee and council meetings. Where strict party discipline operates, it follows that the policy adopted need not represent the will of the majority, but only the will of the majority of the majority – which may well be a minority of the whole. Further, the officers will have less influence on the direction of local affairs if party considerations govern policy and major decisions are taken at private meetings which officers do not attend. Even so, the picture must not be exaggerated. However intense party activity may be, a mass of minor matters remain to be settled by committee debate and by consultation between chief officers and committee chairmen.

## COUNCILLORS

Representative democracy in local government is secured by the regular election of councillors. Excluding parish councillors, there are rather more than 40,000 of them in England and Wales. What type of people are they? The Government Social Survey undertook a detailed investigation of councillors (and aldermen) for the Maud Committee so that we now have a full picture of those who govern us locally. It is clear that they do not constitute a fair cross-section of society. Only 12 per cent of councillors are female. Their average age is fifty-five: women councillors and county and rural district councillors have an even higher average age. A mere 5 per cent of male councillors are below thirty-five, 20 per cent are retired. Certain categories of occupation predominate, employers, managers, professional workers and farmers; this is unsurprising since persons in such occupations are best able to adjust their hours of work to fit in with local authority business. Councillors are immobile; nearly two-thirds say that they have lived in the area they represent for at least twenty-five years. It is comforting that, judged by the test of examination successes, they are better educated than the average of the total population: again it is unsurprising to learn that the youngest councillors are those who have obtained the most academic qualifications. Councillors are also among the most active participants in community affairs and have a high incidence of membership of political parties and other local bodies of all kinds.

We now turn from sociological background to the law. The term of election for councillors is three years but the method of rotating office varies. Counties, London Boroughs and parishes elect councils *en bloc* triennially. In other boroughs one-third of the councillors retire each year. In the districts, urban and rural, there is no uniform practice: the standing arrangement is the same as that for boroughs but, by a two-thirds majority and with the consent of the county council, a district can opt for a local general election every third year. Almost all boroughs are divided into wards and each ward has three councillors, one retiring each year. In counties there is only one representative for each electoral division, so it is impossible to hold an election throughout a county every year. County electoral areas are designed on a single-member basis to keep them as small as possible. The relative advantages of these two systems are worthy of more discussion than they commonly receive. The borough system of annual elections does provide greater continuity of membership for – barring the incidence of casual vacancies – no more than one-third of the councillors can ever be replaced at one time. This is a substantial merit. But the drawbacks to this system are severe. The annual election incurs greater cost and more disturbance to the regular flow of council business. Most boroughs are run on party lines so, if the dominant party has a clear majority on the council, it may be impossible at one annual election to displace the majority group from power even if they are badly beaten at the polls. An election at which the government is immune, at least in the short-term, is not an attractive concept. It must reduce public interest in the right to vote as also does the greater frequency of elections. One advantage claimed for political intervention in local elections is that it increases the turnout of voters. There is no doubt that it does. This makes it even more remarkable that the turnout is always higher in rural district elections than in contests for any other type of authority. Since party activity in rural districts is still low the explanation of the higher voting figures must be that an election is a rare event that arouses public interest. Political parties tend to favour annual elections as these provide the local political organizations with a regular stimulus and help to keep them in better shape for a parliamentary election, especially if this should occur unexpectedly. Annual elections have another important and less recognized consequence. If a council is elected *en bloc* the electoral divisions can be arranged on a single-member basis. So a triennial general election in a borough could permit each ward to be divided into three. With smaller areas and a smaller electorate to canvass, there is a great prospect of individuals unconnected with political parties coming forward to contest the elections and, indeed, of achieving success. Quite obviously there is no reason for the main political parties to advocate a change in the law which would favour independent or minor party candidates.

Another factor which affects the results of elections is the geographical distribution of electoral areas. As the population of an area grows it is necessary to adjust boundaries occasionally to ensure that each councillor represents an approximately equal number of voters. The alteration of ward boundaries in a borough requires an Order-in-Council approving a scheme prepared by a Commissioner nominated by the Home Secretary: in counties the Home Secretary himself can authorize changes: in county districts the county council alters boundaries and an urban district, but not a rural district, has a right of appeal against county council decisions to the Home Secretary. The ability to alter boundaries involves the right to alter the number of councillors. There are, indeed, very large variations in ratios of councillors to the local population. In Lancashire there is one councillor to 14,107 people, in Radnor 1 to 434; county borough extremes are 1 to 4,890 in Sheffield and 1 to 1,357 in Canterbury; urban district extremes are 1 to 3,706 in Basildon and 1 to a mere 102 in Saxmundham. The Maud Committee quoted these figures to support their view that the number of councillors should not exceed 75 in any authority. This may be desirable in the interests of effective management, but in large authorities it would limit the contacts between local administration and the electorate.

Since 1945 all British subjects of either sex aged twenty-one or over have been entitled to the local government franchise unless disqualified by some specific statutory provision, e.g. being a person of unsound mind or a felon. To be able to vote in any area one must have been resident there on the qualifying date and be named on the register of electors: in addition, any owner or tenant of land or premises with a rateable value of at least £10 is also entitled to vote in the area where this property is situated if not entitled to vote there through residential qualification. All local government elections, apart from by-elections, are held in April or May. These dates follow closely on the end of the financial year when the annual rate is fixed. Thus the proximity of elections may affect opinions of councillors when they have to fix the rate level. There can be two views as to whether this is a desirable arrangement.

There are various qualifications governing candidature at local elections. A councillor must be on the register of electors for the area he seeks to represent, or own land within the area or have been resident there for at least twelve months prior to the date of election. People who satisfy these conditions may still be disqualified by any one of the following rules. An employee of a local authority cannot be an elected member of it. Bankruptcy is a disqualification, so is a surcharge of £500 by the district auditor within five years of the election. Those convicted of corrupt practices at elections are barred as well as those convicted for any offence within the last five years for which the penalty imposed was three months or more imprisonment without the option of a fine. Further, a councillor who is absent from council meetings for six months will vacate his seat unless the authority approves his reason for absence.

The foregoing is a summary of the legal position. In many places, however, the overriding condition for membership of the local authority is the ability to obtain party nomination for a seat that the party is likely to win. Necessarily this eliminates those who are not faithful party supporters and those who support a party that is unpopular in the area where they live. There are no reliable statistics to show how far local elections have become dominated by political parties largely because of the ambiguity of the word independent: some 'Independent' councils are controlled by an organization which, if not Conservative, is explicitly anti-Labour, while elsewhere the word 'Independent' implies a lack of declared political views and an absence of any informal organization to govern the council. But there can be no doubt that the party element does restrict the field for recruitment of councillors.

The Maud Committee suggested another disqualification – any person aged seventy or over should be barred from election. Justices of the Peace must already retire from the active list at seventy-five. The analogy is not exact because justices are nominated for life while councillors are subject to triennial re-election. Is age disqualification justified? Certainly, the elderly are less likely to be as vigorous or alert as younger people. On the other hand, should not the electors decide when an individual is unsuitable to represent them? The ability to contest an election successfully is at least some evidence of energy, and many councillors over the age of seventy now give excellent service to local government. Yet the Maud Committee can reply that younger councillors could give even better service.

Perhaps the most intractable constitutional problem affecting councillors (and aldermen) is the relationship between their public duties and their private interests. The law on this subject is governed by Section 76 of the Local Government Act, 1933, as subsequently amended. In essence, the position is that if an elected member has a financial interest in any contract or other matter coming before his authority, he must disclose his interest and not vote or participate in discussion thereon. The interpretation of this provision has caused concern in recent years because it was not clear how small or remote an interest had to be to escape Section 76. An attempt was made to deal with the situation by the Local Government (Pecuniary Interests) Act, 1964, which provides that a member is not to be reguarded as having an interest if it is so remote or insignificant as being unlikely to influence his conduct. Another escape route is that the Minister of Housing and Local Government can issue dispensations to members if the number disabled by the pecuniary interest rule would be so great as to impede the execution of council business. The most common difficulty has been in relation to votes on council rents where Labour would sometimes lose its normal council majority if Labour supporters living in council houses were disqualified. In the past Ministers have sometimes issued temporary dispensations to avoid this occurring and in 1967 the Minister issued Circular 5/67 which announced a general permission for members who are council tenants to speak and vote on housing policy. This does not cover any case concerned with particular properties in which a member may have an interest. All dispensations, while avoiding disqualification, do not remove the need to declare an interest.

Section 76 is decreasingly relevant to the situation. Originally it was designed to ensure that there should be no improper influence exercised by business men who might have contracts with their local authority. Today the threat to probity in local government is quite different. It is that elected members may use 'inside' information about probable future policy in relation to land use for their private advantage. If a member knows that his authority is likely to take certain action which will affect property values, he may make – or encourage relatives, friends or business associates to make – shrewd bargains before the intentions of the authority reach the stage of formal decisions and become public knowledge. Such behaviour is beyond the scope of Section 76. The problem is not that abuse is widespread but rather the virtual impossibility of formulating legislation that would effectively prevent it. To extend to local government some form of Official Secrets Act is at present beyond the bounds of possibility: it would certainly discourage recruitment of councillors. Many authorities have a Standing Order which decrees that committee business shall be treated as confidential until it is communicated to the council or the press, but such an instruction cannot be a watertight safeguard against abuse. A council could decide to exclude from its planning committee any member with interests in business or property; the individual application of such a rule could be very unpleasant, it would deprive the planning committee of useful experience and would not necessarily stop the circulation of valuable information. The best safeguards seem to be the consciences of elected members and the pressure of public opinion.

The discussion of pecuniary interests raises the question of motive. Why do people continue to serve for long periods on local authorities? No authoritative answer to this question is possible. If elected members are asked why they serve, their replies will be highly subjective. Obviously they may be fired by political enthusiasm or be attracted by whatever prestige is associated with the word councillor. It is probably true that most elected members feel that they are doing something useful for the community and, as the Maud Committee noted, the council and its committees become a sort of informal club which the retired members, in particular, find attractive. It is also possible that a few people join local councils out of the hope that financial advantage will be derived therefrom: certainly this is sometimes believed to be so by the general public. Should the idea spread that councillors are in local government for what they can get out of it, persons jealous of their reputation will avoid membership of local authorities. The 'club' would cease to be an attractive one. Here the problem is put bluntly, not because of any immediate prospect that this situation will occur, but because it is a danger not to be overlooked. The maintenance of probity in local government is of the utmost importance from every point of view.

## ALDERMEN

County and borough councils have two categories of members – councillors and aldermen. The aldermen are chosen not at the polls by the electorate but by the councillors. Aldermen constitute one-quarter of a council except in the Greater London Council and the London Boroughs where the proportion is one-sixth. They are elected for a six year term, twice that of a councillor, and half the aldermen are elected each third year: in counties the triennial aldermanic elections are held in the same year as the election of councillors. Voting at an aldermanic election is public in that the votes of individual councillors must be recorded in the minutes. Aldermen are usually selected from among existing councillors, and their election is usually thought of as being an honour or promotion or a reward for past services. Such elections involve the creation of casual vacancies for councillors and cause by-elections to be held. However, it is not inevitable that aldermen be drawn from the councillors: the legal requirement is that an alderman should be *qualified* to be a councillor on the local authority. Thus it is possible to give a council entirely fresh members through the aldermanic system. This was done on the G.L.C. in 1967 when the Conservatives, after their sweeping victory, felt the need to strengthen their ranks by obtaining the services of a few people with great experience. But to introduce outsiders in this way is rare. The advantage of aldermanic status is to confer immunity from the rough-and-tumble of the polls and councillors normally wish to confer this benefit on themselves. There is also an argument for this course in terms of democracy: if the aldermanic system is criticised as undemocratic, it is perhaps less undemocratic to choose those who in the past have won the confidence of the voters than it is to choose those who have not done so.

The law gives aldermen no special duties or privileges as a member of a local authority. In boroughs, but not in counties, the aldermen act as returning officers at elections for councillors. One alderman is allocated to each ward and has to supervise the counting of votes, adjudicate on doubtful votes and decide the election by drawing lots in the unusual event of equality of votes. In any difficult situation an alderman acting as returning officer normally relies on the advice of the Town Clerk. The task of the alderman *qua* alderman is minimal and scarcely makes him indispensable.

The system is open not merely to objection but to abuse. It was introduced into the Municipal Corporations Act, 1835, at the insistence of the House of Lords, to try and strengthen the link between the reformed elected councils and the traditions of the ancient chartered corporations and also as a device to secure some greater continuity of policy and personnel. Where triennial elections are held so that the whole body of councillors may be rejected by the voters, this argument has a little merit; it has no force at all in boroughs where the elections are annual. The dominant fact about aldermen is that they are elderly; over half are above sixty-five years of age. Once elected they tend to be re-elected, unless knocked out by a political convulsion on the council. They are often reluctant to resign in spite of advancing years and declining powers. Both political parties at Sheffield have imposed on themselves a retiring age of seventy for aldermen, but this is an exceptional arrangement.

Aldermen are selected by a variety of criteria. Occasionally the choice is made on purely personal grounds; more often it is based either on seniority or party politics. Where politics dominate the loyalties of council members, aldermanic elections will be settled in a party context: either the majority party will take all, or nearly all, the aldermanic seats, or the parties may come to an agreement to share aldermen proportionately with the number of their councillors. Local arrangements between party groups sometimes break down, and this creates much ill-feeling. Indeed, whatever method of selection is in vogue, an aldermanic election may stimulate personal tension among the members of a local authority – a situation that is not conducive to harmonious concentration upon the essential tasks of local administration. It is not surprising that criticism of the aldermanic system has been common in recent years especially as, due to the growth of the party element in local elections, it can be used in the boroughs to frustrate the will of the electorate. Since aldermanic elections are held every third year, a party that gains a sweeping victory in a non-aldermanic year can obtain no extra aldermen even if a council follows the convention of allocating aldermen between party groups *pro rata* with their councillors. Thus Party A might have a majority of popularly elected councillors while Party B retains an overall majority of council seats through its aldermen. It is even possible in an aldermanic election year for a party with one fewer councillors than its opponents to retain control provided that it has a majority of non-retiring aldermen. The technique works in this way. As non-retiring aldermen may vote in the election of Mayor or County Council Chairman, a party can use these votes to secure the election of one of its own aldermen as Mayor or Chairman. In the following election of aldermen, the occupant of the Chair is entitled to vote; he uses his vote to force a tie, thereupon he uses his casting vote to secure the aldermanic seats for his party colleagues. This blatant abuse, which is entirely legal, has occurred on a few occasions. It certainly adds weight to the case for the abolition of aldermen. The case in their favour is essentially that they assist councils by giving continuity of experience, but this advantage scarcely outweighs the demerits of an undemocratic process, the possibility of party manipulation and of senile influence in public affairs.

The Maud Committee urged that the office of alderman be abolished. If this were done, what would be the effect on local government? Obviously, many present aldermen would drop out of local affairs. The problem is whether this would deprive authorities of the service of valuable members. But an alderman who has insufficient vigour or interest in public affairs to offer himself for election in the normal way is unlikely to make a stimulating contribution to the discussion of public policy. Local government will be healthier and stronger if such people stand aside and open the way for younger minds.

### COUNCIL CHAIRMEN AND MAYORS

The first business at the annual meeting of a local authority is to elect its Chairman and Vice-Chairman or, in the case of a borough, to elect its Mayor. It will be noticed that there is a difference here; a borough council does not choose the Deputy Mayor. The Deputy Mayor is nominated by the Mayor and acts on behalf of the Mayor on various social occasions when the Mayor cannot be present, but the Deputy does not preside over meetings of the borough council in the absence of the Mayor unless specifically asked to do so by the council which may choose instead a temporary chairman from among the aldermen. This technicality of the law is of interest since it serves to stress the two separate aspects of the Mayor's duties. Parliament appears to have felt that, in relation to social duties, the Mayor's deputy should be someone acceptable to him personally, but, in relation to the task of presiding over council business, the person taking the Mayor's place must be acceptable to the council. In fact, most boroughs have evolved a local tradition that governs the choice of Deputy Mayor and in many cases the office is awarded to the out-going Mayor.

A Chairman or Mayor need not be a member of the local authority, but he must be qualified to be a member of it. His period of office is one year; the local conventions about re-election vary but in towns re-election is less usual. He may also be paid a reasonable

allowance to defray the expenses incurred by civic duties for, especially in the boroughs, the amount of social expenditure can be
substantial and it is clearly necessary that recompense should be
paid.

In some other countries the title 'Mayor' describes an official who
has substantial personal responsibilities for the proper conduct of
local administration. The French *maire* is in this position. In the
United States the situation is complicated because there are many
forms of town government and the traditional mayor and council
pattern has often been replaced by other systems thought to be more
efficient or to provide firmer safeguards against corruption, but
where the mayor survives he generally has substantial personal responsibilities, analagous to those of the President in relation to the
Federal Government. The British Mayor has a quite different
position. His executive tasks are minimal. His main formal duty is
to preside at council meetings and ensure that these are conducted
properly in accordance with the rules of council procedure. But
Mayors are always busy people. They are expected to undertake a
formidable programme of appearances at various public occasions,
to entertain distinguished visitors who come to their borough, to
attend civic, cultural and charitable events, school speechdays and
to visit local hospitals, especially on Christmas Day. This whirl of
social activity is punctuated by speeches of welcome and votes of
thanks. The Mayor becomes the embodiment of the community of
the borough. By statute he has precedence over all other persons
save a direct representative of the Crown such as the Lord Lieutenant of the county. The Mayoralty is held in deep respect, but the
respect belongs to the office and not to the man who holds it. This
respect demands that the Mayor abstain from controversial activities – in the same way as the Speaker of the House of Commons:
the general pattern is that the Mayor takes no part in political events
during his period of office. It follows that he does not concern himself with the details of local administration. He does not direct or
supervise borough officers. If important decisions have to be taken
between committee meetings, the responsibility falls on the appropriate committee chairman rather than the Mayor. The normal position is that the Mayor will exercise initiative only in unusual circumstances and then in a non-controversial manner. Thus if there is a
local disaster the Mayor may open a relief fund; by acting in this
way he is not so much providing leadership as expressing the conscience of the community. The Mayoralty, then, is of much civic
significance but does not bestow great influence over local affairs.
Indeed, in some of the larger cities, prominent members of the

majority party group may avoid the office since they prefer to play a leading role in the development of policy, probably through the chairmanship of a major committee.

There is no true parallel between a Mayor and a Chairman of one of the other types of local authority, for the latter are not subjected to such an intense social programme. The Chairman of an Urban District will make a number of public appearances and may wear a chain of office, but the dignity and the status are not the same. On the other hand, a county council Chairman may have more influence than a Mayor. Any generalization on this topic can be misleading. In 'political' counties the leader of the majority party may be Chairman of the council and when the Chairman of a non-political county council is re-elected year after year one suspects that he has developed a position of real power.

## OFFICERS

The term 'local government officer' creates a mind-picture of people who work at desks in the local town hall or county hall. In fact, office-workers form but a fraction of the total employees of local authorities. Not only do local councils need the services of a large 'outdoor' manual staff concerned largely with cleansing operations and construction work, but a wide variety of skills are also required, e.g. teachers, policemen, welfare workers, if all local government duties are to be carried out effectively. But the administrative and clerical staff in the local offices are at the heart of the administrative system and for this reason demand special attention.

The days when the parish, as the most important unit of local government, could rely on the services of part-time unpaid officers are long past. Elected members have neither the time nor the range of professional expertise necessary to direct all the business of a local authority. Parliament has therefore insisted that certain officers be appointed. Each county, borough and district must have a Clerk, Treasurer and Medical Officer of Health; all, except a rural district, must have a Surveyor; all, except a county, must have a Public Health Inspector. Each local education authority must appoint a Chief Education Officer; each county and county borough must appoint a Children's Officer. Each police authority must have a Chief Constable. These legal provisions have historial significance in that they recall some unwillingness in the nineteenth-century to make certain appointments, notably in relation to health. Today they help to create a uniformity in the pattern of local authority departments, but the number of officers appointed is far in excess of the statutory requirement. This can be illustrated by example: a county council must appoint a Clerk, but is not required by law to give him any assistants – yet in few counties will the staff in the Clerk's Department fail to approach a hundred. Another feature of the law is that Parliament has not decreed that these statutory officers be full-time appointments. Part-time service is limited to the smallest authorities and is steadily declining, but it is still not unknown for two small adjacent district councils to share a clerk. The jobs of clerk and the treasurer must not be combined although a small authority may save money by appointing a clerk-cum-chief-financial-officer and ask a local bank manager to fill the statutory office of treasurer. Once the structure of local government has been reorganized all these arrangements will be swept away.

Each local authority appoints its own staff who hold office, subject to exceptions noted below, at the pleasure of the council. There is a convention that officers are not normally dismissed except for serious misconduct, but a council cannot be expected to retain the services of a chief officer if it has no faith in his judgment or suitability to hold a post of responsibility. Some officers, however, are liable to incur the hostility of influential people if their duties are carried out rigorously, so the law gives them special protection. Thus a Chief Constable, a Medical Officer of Health and a Public Health Inspector cannot be dismissed without Ministerial consent. The same is true for the Clerk of a county council. Any policeman who is dismissed or required to resign can appeal to the Home Secretary. The overall position of local government officers is tolerably secure, not so much because of legal provisions, but because of public conscience and the strength of trade unionism in local government. When the structure of authorities in the London area was reshaped in 1963 great care was taken to safeguard the interests of officers whose position was affected by the reorganization.

Ministerial control over appointments is also used in a few cases to prevent the selection of anyone felt to be unsuitable. The Secretary of State for Education and Science has a veto power over the choice of a Chief Education Officer and the Home Secretary has similar power over the post of children's officer. The Home Secretary must approve the nomination of Chief Constables; there have been cases where this approval has been withheld because it was proposed to fill a vacancy by internal promotion within the local force. Similarly, he must approve the appointment of Chief Fire Officers. Whether controls of this nature are necessary or desirable is a matter of controversy. If a local authority is regarded by Parliament as being fully capable of choosing a suitable Clerk or Treasurer – why is it not capable of choosing a Chief Education Officer?

The major safeguard against bad appointments is the requirement that officers in positions of responsibility should have appropriate professional qualifications. Sometimes this stipulation has a statutory basis, otherwise it is conventional or included in the schedule of agreements made through the Whitley machinery governing pay and conditions of service for local government officers. This demand for professional qualifications has certain effects on the recruitment of staff which are discussed in Chapter VII, but they are valuable in that they ensure a minimum quality of proficiency and obviate much of the possibility of corruption in making appointments. Another feature of the local government service is that promotion is obtained through moving from place to place gaining wider experience of different conditions. There is also a tendency to choose officers from another authority of the same type, so the common practice is to move from one borough to another, from one county to another and so on. This produces in an officer not merely a sense of loyalty to his employing authority but a loyalty to his type of authority. Again, there can be two opinions as to whether this is a desirable condition.

The central issue which affects senior local government officers is the nature of their relationship with their employing authority – how far can officers persuade elected members to accede to their views? In law, there is no problem. A council decides policy and instructs its officers to carry out its wishes; officers, as servants of the council, must obey. However, in conformity with the general law of master and servant, a local government officer cannot escape the consequences of an illegal act by pleading that he was acting under the instructions of his council. In a notable application of this principle the courts have held (*Attorney General v. De Winton, 1906*) that a Borough Treasurer must disobey an order from his council that calls for an illegal payment; the argument here is that a Borough Treasurer is not a mere servant of his council but has a fiduciary responsibility to the burgesses as a whole. If a Treasurer refused to carry out an instruction from his council because of doubts about its legality, it would still be open to the council, at least in theory, to dismiss their Treasurer. If ever a dispute threatened to reach this stage, public opinion would be aroused and play a large part in deciding the issue. There is no parallel ruling governing the position of a Clerk if faced with what he feels to be an illegal instruction. All that can be said is that if a Clerk wishes to secure his position against a possible surcharge by the District Auditor, he must at least ensure that the dubious instruction is given by the council as a whole and not merely by an influential member or group of members, (*Re Hurle-Hobbs ex parte Riley and another, 1944*).

The inferior status of officers is symbolized by some authorities through the seating arrangements in their council chamber, for the Clerk (or Town Clerk) sits immediately below the dias where the Chairman (or Mayor) presides over council meetings. This layout is extremely inconvenient whenever the Chairman wishes to consult the Clerk. Elsewhere the Clerk is permitted to sit on the left hand side of the Chair; this makes it easy, perhaps too easy, for the Clerk to offer advice. Most Clerks are unhappy about proffering advice at a public council meeting except on matters of procedure where the need may be simply to remind the council of their own standing orders. The Clerk and other officers prefer to advise in the privacy of committee meetings. Necessarily the officers have a store of information which elected members would be foolish to ignore. Officers can draw upon a lifetime of professional experience and will know, or should know, not merely the legal, financial and technical complications of matters that come before committees, but the various Ministerial rulings and advice as set out in Departmental Circulars and other official publications. Obviously, an official may present factual information in such a way as to lead elected members towards the policy he thinks best. But advice must always be presented tactfully. A committee resents an official who appears overbearing or impatient. A wise officer knows that a committee should always feel that it has itself made the decisions. The influence of officers tends to be greatest where an authority meets least frequently and where it is not controlled by a political group: these conditions apply to many county councils. Officers view the advent of party politics in local government with mixed feelings. On the one hand, it reduces the impact they can make on policy; on the other, it probably assists continuity and certainty of policy, for once the dominant group has decided upon a course of action it is loath to retract. The party element also strengthens the need for local government officers, like civil servants, to be non-political. Where one party has controlled an authority for many years there is a danger that chief officers will be identified with the ruling party – a situation that can cause great difficulty should the party control change hands. It follows that aspiring politicians should not seek to become local government officers. Clerks (or Town Clerks) and their deputies are specifically disqualified from membership of the House of Commons; this disqualification does not extend to other local government officers but it is rare for local authority employees, other than teachers, to attain political prominence.

The Clerk, above all other officials, is in a strong position to exert influence. He is expected to provide legal advice on all aspects of council affairs and through the committee clerks on his staff he is in constant touch with all details of business. Even so, much depends on the personality of the individual Clerk. If he is respected because of his ability and other personal qualities, he will be consulted regularly by other chief officers and possibly by committee chairmen. If he is disliked or feared, his influence will be less and certainly will be achieved less happily. It is increasingly accepted that the Clerk should have overall responsibility for the co-ordination and efficiency of his authority's administration – a topic discussed more fully in Chapter VII. While these responsibilities are theoretically separate from control of policy, in practice, the division is not clear-cut. Inevitably, the wider administrative responsibilities of the Clerk give him a position of primacy over other chief officers and again enhances his ability to exercise influence. Yet the most successful Clerks recognize that their main duty is to interpret the mind of their local authority rather than to mould it.

## STANDING ORDERS

Methods of procedure in local government are necessarily more complex, some would say clumsy, than the administrative processes in industry or commerce. Since local authorities spend public money they have a special duty to see that it is properly spent: risks which are commonly taken by private enterprise are less acceptable in public administration. The other difference is that local councils reach decisions after discussion, much of which is held in public, because in a democracy the public have a right to know how public business is being conducted. So to ensure that their affairs are conducted in a regular and orderly manner, local authorities draw up Standing Orders to regulate their own conduct. These are in addition to the statutory controls in the law of local government and they must not, of course, transgress statutory provisions.

Standing Orders are mainly concerned with laying down rules of debate and with the procedure for using the council seal and for dealing with tenders and contracts. The form of Standing Orders varies very much between authorities so that no detailed description would have general application. However, they will always govern the order of business at council meetings and how various types of motion or amendment may be moved. Some councils impose a time limit on speeches. This raises a number of issues: how much time should each member be given; how much preferential treatment, if any, should be given to the chairman of a committee or the mover of a motion; how far should there be a right of reply? It is much better to avoid any time limits but this may not be possible in large authorities or where debates are animated by political differences. The major item of business at a normal council meeting is the consideration of minutes or reports from committees. Again, this can be organized in at least two different ways. Committee chairmen may present their minutes or reports in turn and any questions or arguments about committee proposals may be allowed when the council are asked to approve them paragraph by paragraph. The danger of this method is that the council may spend an excessive amount of time on the affairs of those committees which happen to come early on the agenda. To try to obviate this imbalance of attention, Standing Orders may lay down an alternative procedure. This often takes the form of requiring the Clerk to read through the numbers of the paragraphs of each committee report: a member may interrupt to ask a committee chairman a question on the contents of a paragraph, but if he wishes to start an argument and challenge policy, he will say simply 'Object'. Then when the Clerk has finished reading through the paragraph numbers, the council proceeds to discuss the items to which objection has been taken. In this way members can get a conspectus of the total amount of contentious business before them and this may help them to use debating time more sparingly and effectively. Standing Orders can also guard against another danger – that a council will be rushed into hasty decisions without adequate prior consideration. There is a statutory rule that a county or borough council cannot consider any business unless it has been specified in a notice summoning the meeting sent out three days in advance. This rule does not apply to district councils or to committees, but may be imposed by local Standing Orders. Regarding contracts, Standing Orders prescribe how tenders shall be invited and how they shall be submitted. A general instruction is that the amount of a tender must be treated as confidential to ensure genuine competition among contractors. Contractors may be expected to apply Fair Wages conditions to their employees, observe specifications issued by the British Standards Institution and use British or Commonwealth materials wherever possible. It is also common for an authority's Standing Orders to define the extent and conditions of powers delegated to committees. A borough or county may also include rules governing the election of aldermen which are supplementary to, and must be in accordance with, the relevant statutory provisions.

Standing Orders are a vital element in the constitution of a local authority. They help to ensure harmonious operation and financial regularity. It is, of course, essential that they are understood both by elected members and by officers in positions of responsibility. Officers must observe the detailed regulations covering contracts and financial management; elected members will not be able to play a full part in discussion unless they know when and how they may intervene.

# Chapter VI

# COMMITTEES

Even in the smallest local authorities – other than parishes – it is obvious that all the detailed consideration of business cannot be done at meetings of the full council. Accordingly, committees are established. The tendency is for them to grow in number and in authority. They consume a great amount of time of both elected members and officers. It it commonly said that the committee is the workshop of local government: certainly, a realistic appraisal of committee behaviour is essential to a full understanding of the practice of local administration.

### THE STRUCTURE OF COMMITTEE ACTIVITY

Committees may be classified in two ways, according to their legal status or according to the nature of their function. The legal distinction is between those that are required to exist by statute and those created at the will of the local council. In the case of many major services, committees are mandatory. Each local education authority must have an Education Committee; every county and county borough must have a Health Committee and a Welfare Services Committee. County councils must have Finance Committees – boroughs need not, although they always do have one. Parliament has insisted that these 'statutory' committees be appointed in order to secure that the functions connected with them are the particular concern of certain members of the council and are not treated as matters of secondary importance. The idea of a statutory committee embodies an unjustified lack of trust in local authorities and is an example of a legal restraint on local government that could well be repealed. It is inconceivable that any local education authority would consider this function too insignificant to justify the establishment of a separate committee.

The other distinction is of greater practical importance. Some committees have charge of a particular sector of a council's work, e.g. housing, health, education, and these are sometimes known as 'vertical' committees. The other type of committee has 'horizontal' duties – it deals with one aspect of council activity across the whole range of its functions; the Finance Committee is the leading example and others are a Works Committee or an Establishment Committee. Vertical bodies tend to deal only with one department of the local authority; the Education Committee supervises the education department, the Health Committee supervises the health department and so on. Horizontal bodies are concerned with all departments of the authority and have some responsibility for co-ordinating the actions of their vertical associates. Most committees are standing committees in that they are assumed to be permanent and are re-appointed each year, but special *ad hoc* committees can be nominated on a temporary basis to deal with a particular problem.

The number of committees varies considerably; naturally small authorities tend to have fewer than large authorities. Even so, the range is substantial. The Maud Committee discovered that in county councils the total could be as low as 12 or as high as 29, while in county boroughs the limits were 12 and 35. To these must be added sub-committees which averaged 47 in county councils and 40 in county boroughs. In second-tier authorities, with fewer functions to perform, the committee structure is less complex, although again there are wide variations. As county councils have a tradition of quarterly meetings, the frequency of their committees is somewhat less. But every councillor knows that the routine time-table of meetings is supplemented by others called for a special purpose, e.g. to make a visit or to appoint an officer or teacher. When a local authority acquires a new task that does not fit squarely into the sphere of an existing committee, there will be a temptation to form a new body to deal with it. This is very likely to happen should the new function fall half-way between the interests of two existing committees; in these circumstances if the extra duty is given to one committee, the other will be offended. The creation of a new body provides a tolerable compromise at the cost of more people spending more time at more meetings. Similarly, a committee faced with an extra type of business may too easily establish a new sub-committee. The other danger is that committees once born become unwilling to die. It may be justifiable to have a separate body to consider a fresh and unexplored problem but, if the new category of business contracts or becomes routine, the justification disappears. A council should review its committee structure regularly, say at three-year intervals, and ruthlessly cut out decaying parts and effect amalgamations wherever possible.

Each local authority decides on the size of its committees. The larger the body, the wider the range of opinion and experience that can be represented on it. Conversely, the larger the body the smaller must be the scope for the average member to play a significant part in its work and the greater will be the cost in terms of time demanded of the elected members. Authorities in rural areas tend to have larger committees because there is pressure for the constituent geographical parts to be represented. In rural district councils where a parish has but a single representative, he or she may feel compelled to serve on all the R.D.C. committees, otherwise the interests of the parish may be overlooked. The Maud Report showed that over half the finance committees of county councils had between 20 and 29 members whereas in nearly three-quarters of county boroughs the parallel figure was between 10 and 19. Similarly county education committees are larger than those of county boroughs and 82 per cent of them have at least 40 members. The more important committees are often large in size because members are keen to serve on them, and while optimum size must be a matter of opinion, those in local government are mostly too big, notably county education committees. Where each parish wishes to be included on rural district committees the latter become virtually synonymous with the full council. This at least has the merit of reducing the length of council meetings.

A special committee is often nominated to allocate council members to the various committees. This is clearly a delicate, personal operation and may be affected by a number of principles. Where a council is run on party lines the majority group will ensure that it has a political majority on each committee. Otherwise the interests and experience of members are taken into account, also their regularity of attendance and reputation with fellow council members. The finance committee is the key committee of a council and the most senior and able members are usually selected to serve on it. New councillors frequently complain that they are relegated to committees of second-rank importance.

Would it be useful for local authorities to inject more outside blood into their proceedings? The law permits this to be done. A council may include on its committees (other than a finance committee) persons with full voting rights who are not members of the parent council, providing that such additional members do not form more than one-third of any committee. This practice of co-option from outside does enable local authorities to widen the range of specialized knowledge and experience available for their deliberations. Under the Allotments Act, 1922, such additional members must be included on allotment committees. Magistrates form one-third of every Police Authority but this is tantamount to the creation of a joint committee rather than co-option. Elsewhere, co-option is optional. It is commonly used on education committees and boards of school governors and managers. (There is a widespread misconception that co-opted members are mandatory for education committees.) But apart from allotments and education, this device is not much used. One reason is a feeling that it is undemocratic to give authority to persons who have not been popularly elected. Council members may think that they can get adequate specialized advice from their officers. They may also fear that co-opted members would out-shine them in discussion and have an unduly dominant role in committee decisions. Critics have also said that the system can be abused – that where councils are run on political lines, co-option can be a method of compensation for defeated council candidates; in fact, this happens but rarely. Granted that the law provides adequate safeguards, the practice of bringing additional people into local committee work is valuable and should perhaps be used more widely.

Meetings of committees are held in an informal atmosphere. The chief officers responsible for the committee's business or a committee clerk will sit next to the Chairman in a strategic position to offer *sotto voce* words of advice. If the body is small enough it will sit round a table. Smoking is permitted unless the warnings of the Ministry of Health have had effect. At the first meeting of the council year the initial task is to elect a Chairman. Where a council is subject to political control the Chairman is chosen by the majority group – otherwise the choice depends on the interplay of personalities. At other meetings normal practice is to start by approving the minutes of the previous meeting. The other items on the agenda will be to consider developments in matters that have been previously before the committee, and new pieces of business. Information on these will either have been circulated beforehand in reports prepared by the officers or there will be a verbal report at the meeting. Subcommittee reports are usually introduced by the chairmen of subcommittees. The volume of papers circulated to members to prepare them for the business varies considerably; often it is very substantial. The Maud Report noted that one of the largest county boroughs sent out 700 sheets of paper a month to each member of the council and 1,000 sheets to those on the education committee. One wonders what proportion of the papers are read.

There is no doubt that members are kept well informed about the business of the committees on which they serve. In the case of education, the status of the committee is protected by law: a local education authority is required by statute to refer all matters to its education committee and must consider the committee's recommendations before taking action, except in an emergency. Committees are no longer used for purely advisory purposes. Authority to make final decisions is delegated to them on an increasing scale in order to speed up the flow of council business. The degree of delegation is greatest in large authorities, especially in county councils. Where a council is run on party lines it may arrange that, subject to statutory restrictions, all relevant powers shall be delegated to each committee provided it is unanimous; if all parties agree, there can be no reason to delay the execution of a committee decision. Often delegation is governed, at least in part, by convention rather than precise rules. The Clerk of a large Urban District explained to me that his authority permitted a great deal of delegation to committees but that there were no written regulations about it as the council was unlikely to accept such rules. It seemed that the arrangement was for the Clerk to authorize immediate action on committee decisions apart from those items which he thought so important or potentially controversial as to be likely to arouse comment at a council meeting. No doubt, this amount of informality is exceptional. Yet there is still much rule-of-thumb governing delegation to committees and, indeed, to officers. Especially with education the volume of detail is so great that a high level of delegation is inescapable. An education committee tends to become a separate authority, save that its expenditure must be approved by the finance committee and that major questions of educational policy may be discussed at council meetings.

It follows that the content of committee work is mixed. Sometimes issues of general policy are discussed and recommendations formulated for presentation to the full council. Much of the time is spent, however, in making decisions on administrative matters that fall within the ambit of an accepted policy.

One other curious feature of committee work is worthy of mention. A committee tends to spend approximately the same amount of time over each of its meetings. The period may vary from one and a half hours to five hours, but once a traditional period is established, members adhere to it. If an agenda is unusually heavy, discussion is hurried along; if an agenda is thin, deliberation lingers on points of detail. While this is inefficient it is also very human. Should a meeting last longer than usual, members either have to leave before the end or be late for subsequent appointments – or a meal. When a meeting finishes early members may not know how to spend the time saved; they may even feel that a short meeting implies that they have not done their duty.

## CONTROL OF COMMITTEES

It has been shown that committees are separate but inter-related cogs in the local government machine. How can they be made to mesh smoothly together? This raises the allied problems of co-ordination and control. Such supervision is essential otherwise committees would become wholly independent entities. Control is vital to ensure that a council remains in full charge of its policies and expenditure, and this must often involve a straight refusal to accept committee proposals. Co-ordination is needed to prevent waste. It need not involve saying 'No' to a committee, but is rather a matter of showing them that their proposals can be carried out more satisfactorily or economically if they are done in a certain way. There is an obvious advantage in relating road breaking and road-repair schedules. One committee may find that a certain piece of land or property is surplus to requirements while another committee may be seeking to buy a similar property. At this level progress may be assisted by elected members who serve on two or more committees with overlapping interests. In the larger authorities, however, co-ordination is increasingly the responsibility of chief officers. At lower levels, e.g. the need to maintain steady work flows for office and outdoor staff, the responsibility must rest wholly on officials, especially the Clerk. The question of how far this administrative co-ordination is adequate will be considered more fully below.

Committees cannot apply the council seal to legal documents without the council's consent. There are also a number of financial restraints on their activities. By law they are prohibited from levying a rate or raising a loan. Their annual estimates of expenditure go before the finance committee and are then presented to the council for approval. Any excess of expenditure over the sums approved in the estimates will require the submission of supplementary estimates. In the past Parliament has been excessively fearful of the spending habits of county council committees: under the Local Government Act, 1933, a county could not incur a liability of more than £50 without first receiving an estimate from its finance committee, an amount raised to £100 by the Local Government Act, 1948. These provisions were criticized as unduly restrictive by the Local Government Manpower Committee and were repealed in 1958. This little piece of local government history is symptomatic of hostility towards any independence of committees. Further, all committee spending is subject to review by auditors, internal and external, who provide a rigorous check against irregularity.

Control of committee policy raises other issues. It is important that this should not be heavy-handed and be broadly restricted to supervision of major items, otherwise committees will lose their sense of responsibility and there will be delay while all proposals wait to be ratified by the whole council.

The formal process of control takes place at council meetings at which reports or minutes of committees are presented for approval. Where a committee has delegated powers it will present a report of its actions for the information of council members and not for approval. Practice varies as to how detailed these reports are. For obvious reasons in the larger authorities the scale of delegation is greater and less detail can be included in reports if they are not to be unduly lengthy. At the full council meeting should members object to the way in which delegated powers have been exercised they can do nothing where the delegation is absolute, but some authorities allow a delegated decision to be countermanded if it has not already been put into effect. Of course, the ultimate weapon of the council would be to withdraw the delegation.

On matters that are not delegated the council can always reject a committee's proposals or refer them back for further consideration. This occurs in but a limited number of cases. Time at council meetings is not limited in any strict or formal sense, but the patience and energy of elected members are limited. Were a large number of recommendations to be challenged, then meetings would become unduly long. In general, councils have confidence in their committees. There is little point in forming them if the full body of members insists in doing the work all over again. When a committee's view is challenged its chairman should be better informed than his critics and in a good position to win the argument.

Even so, there will be many occasions when the specialized enthusiasms of a committee will be overruled on matters of principle, on issues that affect the business of other committees and especially on levels of expenditure. How is this done? Wherever a council is run on party lines, policy supervision can be expected to come from the dominant political group which will settle its internal disputes, if necessary, by vote at its 'caucus' meetings. In the absence of strong party loyalties, the situation becomes more flexible. The finance committee can normally persuade a council to prune back any proposals for expenditure it considers excessive. Otherwise the check to a committee is imposed by the balance of opinion as expressed in council debate. It is obvious that a council must always prevail in any fundamental clash with a committee because it holds the ultimate sanction of being able to replace recalcitrant committee members with others who will heed the views of the full council.

## A CRITIQUE OF COMMITTEE WORK

The committee system offers substantial advantages. It ensures that all business has been subjected to prior consideration before it comes to a council meeting and thus avoids hasty decisions. This process of pre-digestion should enable a council to devote its attention to matters of major importance. Council members can specialize on particular aspects of the authority's work, thus helping them to make a valuable contribution to it. The specialization also leads to a deeper sense of involvement and commitment; it heightens the sense of responsibility for the committee's work. And by narrowing the ambit of concentration for the elected member, the committee system enhances his education in administration. The informal atmosphere softens differentials in status and partisan opinions. So officers can intervene in discussion and offer advice to an extent that would be resented and thought improper at council meetings. And where a local authority is dominated by party loyalty, in the freedom of committee the members will not always talk and act in party groupings.

Since a council cannot take all decisions one obvious alternative is to transfer much decision-making power to an individual, be he official or elected member. But the wisdom of any one man (or woman) acting alone is open to doubt, quite apart from the force of the dictum that power corrupts. The committee enables power to be shared and brings together a variety of interests and experience which, in most cases, should produce a better and more acceptable decision. Not all members will play an equal part in moulding the collective mind of the meeting: there will be always a few who give a lead, either through stronger personality or greater experience and ability. An adviser to the committee, a chief officer, may almost always persuade it. In these circumstances a committee decision is perhaps not a genuine collective decision, but is rather a 'front' or support for those people who dominate its deliberations. Yet a committee, unless completely inert, is a valuable check. The leading voices still have to convince. Without committees, far more decisions would be made without potential challenge.

Equally committees are open to criticism. There must be a tendency for each one to live in a world of its own, deeply conscious of its special problems but failing to see them in the context of the full responsibilities of the council. They may be swayed too easily by the advice of officials, backed by the authority of professional qualifications, which can produce undue enthusiasm and ill-balanced judgment. As a committee becomes a separate entity it may seek to build an empire and be over-concerned with matters of status. The multiplicity of committees means also that some matters may need to come before two or more of them for consideration; if they disagree, time and energy may have to be spent in resolving the difference. When sub-committees are not given power to act, items of business will be considered twice, involving duplication of effort. In general, there is a lack of unity about the work of local authorities, and basically the separatism is caused by departmental loyalties stimulated further through the committee system.

There is also a lack of definition of what committees are supposed to do. Again, this is a matter that varies between authorities and is determined by local conventions. Everywhere committees are concerned with the formulation of general policy to be presented to the parent council and give detailed attention to finance. Beyond that there is no uniform practice. It was noted above that the power to delegate decisions to the committees is widely used, especially in counties. But how far should committees themselves deal with the detailed application of general policy, or how far should these matters be left to officials? Again, the extent to which officials are permitted to act will vary. In larger authorities, delegation to officials has increased both in order to save time and to prevent committees being overburdened with detail. But except perhaps in county councils, the elected representatives tend to be unwilling to surrender their prerogatives. At least three reasons contribute to this reluctance. There is a widespread conception of democracy, dating from the Victorian era, which insists that it is the duty of elected representatives to take all decisions; that it is undemocratic to allow officials to exercise discretion. Legal provisions also support this attitude: the Local Government Act, 1933, Third Schedule, part V, paragraph 1, reads, '. . . all acts of a local authority and all questions coming or arising before a local authority shall be done and decided by a majority of the members of a local authority present and voting thereon at a meeting of the local authority'. As we have seen, delegation to committees is permitted by statute but the law is silent about delegation to officers. A further principle of law, *delegatus non potest delegare*, a delegate is unable to delegate, acts as a further restraint on the formal handing down of authority. Finally, there is the undoubted fact that many councillors do not wish to surrender matters to officials because they like dealing with details and personal cases.

A substantial cost has to be paid for this insistence that elected representatives must take decisions. Committee meetings are lengthy; sub-committees multiply; mounds of paper are distributed to explain the detailed business to committee members; officials spend much time in preparing these papers; if they are conscientious, committee members must spend much time on studying agendas and reports; decisions are delayed until committees, and sometimes the full council, have met. All this might be tolerable were it certain that decisions are made under optimum conditions. Unhappily this is not the case. Often elected representatives may be less qualified to take decisions than the officers who advise them. This statement has an undemocratic flavour but frequently it must be true. Normally a happy marriage between democratic principle and expertise is possible since committees accept the advice of their professional staff. A committee would not dispute the view of its surveyor that a bridge was unsafe. School governors and managers commonly think it improper to intervene on questions of curriculum. Yet this self-denying convention may break down. What is the best course of action to take in relation to a child in care? Here any member of a Children's Committee may feel that his opinion is as valuable as that of the Children's Officer. When a committee is faced with an aesthetic issue it is a matter for argument whether professional advice should necessarily be followed. There is great variety in the extent to which elected members concern themselves with staff appointments, including teachers: it is arguable that this is a type of responsibility that chief officials should be expected to shoulder. There is a danger that when committee members become involved in personal cases emotion may determine action, or an undesirable element of patronage or even corruption may creep into council business. Housing is an obvious example. If council tenancies are decided by officials operating a points scheme, no favouritism is likely to arise; if a housing committee or sub-committee arranges tenancies, the basis of decisions becomes a matter for speculation.

Perhaps the most damaging criticism of the present system is that the concentration on detail gives elected representatives inadequate time to concentrate on major matters of policy. Committee members snowed under with papers containing information on trivial matters will have less time to read more important documents, e.g. Ministry circulars. Indeed, where circulars are not immediately relevant to committee business, members may never know of the existence of a circular or will not appreciate its contents. Likewise at meetings, if hours are consumed by the minor items on the agenda, inadequate time is left for important business. A wily official may put a difficult matter of policy at the end of an agenda in the hope that he can persuade a tired committee to follow a certain line of action. It is the case that some committees, the weak committees, prefer to take time over fairly routine items and then get through the major business rapidly by following the advice of their staff because the major items are too complex for members to be able to debate effectively.

In theory, one can argue that committees should decide policy and leave their officials to carry out the details of administration. In practice, the distinction between policy and administration can never be clear-cut. At what stage does a decision on how to put a policy into practice become itself a policy decision? If unexpected administrative difficulties develop which involve additional expenditure, the elected representatives must be consulted. If the operation of a policy incurs unexpected difficulties with the public, the councillors will need to know. And in the smaller authorities if all administrative matters disappeared from committee agendas, there would often be inadequate business to justify holding meetings. No doubt, meetings could be held less frequently but at the cost of further delay to remaining business.

As local authorities come to have wider functions and as the authorities tend to become fewer in number and larger in size, councillors must place increasing trust on the judgment of their officers. This principle is now widely admitted, even where the need for it is regretted. But not all the problems raised in this chapter can be solved by leaving matters to officials. The proposals of the Maud Committee for a drastic overhaul of the nature of committee work are discussed in the next chapter.

---

# Chapter VII

# THE QUEST FOR EFFICIENCY

In March, 1964, the Minister of Housing and Local Government appointed two committees of enquiry into local government at the request of four local authority associations, the Association of Municipal Corporations, the County Councils Association, the Urban District Councils Association and the Rural District Councils Association. One committee, with Sir George Mallaby as Chairman, was required to investigate the staffing of local government. The other had wider terms of reference: 'to consider in the light of modern conditions how local government might best continue to attract and retain people (both elected representatives and principal officers) of the calibre necessary to ensure its maximum effectiveness'. Under the guidance of its Chairman Sir John Maud (now Lord Redcliffe-Maud) this committee undertook a far-reaching investigation into the management of local authorities. Both committees reported in 1967 and these important documents will be discussed more fully below. As a preliminary it must be noted that the mere fact that these two enquiries were set in motion does indicate a widespread malaise about local government: indeed, the terms of reference clearly imply concern about the quality of the *people* in local government. No great institution can be efficient if those who work for it have limited ability or poor morale and if the public 'image' of the institution deters other more suitable persons from coming forward to help with the work. The Maud Committee proposed fundamental reforms in the internal organization of local authorities because it felt that if councillors and officials were frustrated by petty and time-wasting methods of doing business, then able people would be less willing to concern themselves with the management of local public affairs.

The phrase 'reform of local government' has traditionally been associated with discussions about the geographical area of local authorities, and the distribution of functions between upper-tier and lower-tier authorities. Today, other types of reform, reforms of

procedures, of councillor-official relationships, of staffing arrangements and of management techniques, are at least as pressing. They
may well attract less public discussion because such issues are
specialized and arouse far less emotion than the alteration of a
county boundary. But for those engaged in local government the
importance of management reform needs no emphasis.

### STAFF RECRUITMENT AND TRAINING

The officers of local authorities do not constitute a single body, such
as the Civil Service, employed by one master. Each authority deter-
mines its own establishment of staff and appoints its own officers.
Except in those instances (already noticed) in which appointment or
dismissal is subject to Ministerial consent, and in the few cases in
which there is some central prescription of qualifications, e.g. Medical Officers and Public Health Inspectors, each authority is free to
recruit its officers in its own way, and to impose what qualifications
it desires. Nevertheless, the whole body of local government officers
possesses many uniform characteristics and has in recent years con-
formed in increasing measure to standards and uniformities introduced into pay, service conditions, entry and promotion tests, and
many other elements in the officer's contract of service with his
employing authority. These developments are due, partly to trade
union organization among the staffs themselves, and partly and more
recently to joint organization of both the staffs and the local authorities in Whitley machinery for collective bargaining. The local government officers trade union NALGO persuaded Parliament to pass
legislation in 1937 to establish a unified superannuation scheme for
local government. This facilitated the movement of officers between
authorities, opened up better promotion prospects and enabled officers to acquire a wider range of experience. In the inter-war period
NALGO also struggled hard to establish Whitley machinery, i.e. to
create joint consultation with employers over questions of pay and
conditions of service. While such consultation was operative in some
areas, it was not until 1944 that a National Joint Council was established with the agreement of the associations of local authorities.
The National Joint Council is supplemented by Provincial Councils
which deal with local problems. In 1946 the N.J.C. approved a
national scheme of salaries and service conditions, known as 'the
charter', providing a framework of scales for the grading of posts.
This is now operative throughout the country and it has in part been
supplemented by agreements for standard gradings among certain
classes of officer. More recently still special negotiating committees
have agreed upon scales of pay and standard conditions of service

for the chief officers of local authorities who fall outside the National Joint Council's purview.

The Whitley machinery also became responsible for settling standards of recruitment, training and qualification. It enlisted the help of university staff, the governing bodies of the professions and the various occupational groups of the service in deciding the standards to be enforced. This policy was implemented by the N.J.C. by the establishment, under its auspices, of a Local Government Examinations Board. This Board had advisory functions on questions of education, qualifications and training and also organized examinations, the syllabuses for which concentrated on government and administration. Three levels of examination were arranged as the Clerical examination, and the intermediate and final stages of the Diploma in Municipal Administration. Success at these examinations (or in obtaining equivalent qualifications offered by professional bodies) became a prerequisite, but not a guarantee, of advancing beyond certain grades in the local government hierarchy.

Local government is now open to the criticism that it is examination ridden. Yet this emphasis on paper qualifications has ensured a high level of professional competence among officials. It has also done much to eliminate canvassing or corruption in the making of local appointments.

These arrangements for recruitment and training were, no doubt, less than perfect but still worked tolerably well until the nineteen-sixties presented local authorities with a fresh kind of staffing problem – their ability to attract and retain staff of adequate calibre. In earlier years this had presented no difficulty. Boys from the grammar schools had been keen to enter local government because it offered both security and prospects of promotion to positions of respect in society. After entry young men studied for various professional examinations and obtained promotion by moving round from one authority to another, and in due course the most able of them became senior officials. (The Medical Officers and Directors of Education were exceptions to this pattern as they are required to have university training.) Thus the local authorities had no worries about the quality of their staff as the grammar schools provided a steady flow of excellent recruits. Now this source of supply is less fruitful since an increasing proportion of young people with good G.C.E. results leave school to follow various kinds of further education – at universities, colleges of technology, teacher training colleges, etc. Few are left for local government, so the quality of local government entrants has fallen considerably. It becomes a matter of doubt as to how many of those now entering the local government service have the ability to succeed in the professional examinations or, indeed, have the personal qualities required to make a first-rate chief officer. This problem is not unique to local government. It faces other professions that have traditionally recruited school-leavers. But local authorities appear to be in greater difficulty, perhaps because their 'image' seems dull and uninspiring. This is not to assert that local government is dull and uninspiring. Like beauty, the image of local government is in the eye of the beholder.

Essentially this is the situation that faced the Mallaby Committee. Its central recommendations were predictable. Local authorities should improve their liaison arrangements with schools to show school-leavers that local administration offers an attractive and worthwhile career. Also they must recruit more university graduates and make the best possible use of the abilities of their staff. So the Mallaby Committee proposed various developments in post-entry training for staff, ranging from induction training for junior entrants to management training for senior staff. At the local level the Clerk of the authority should have an overall responsibility for establishment work including training; at the national level the Committee proposed the creation of a Local Government Training Board which should both exercise some general supervision over the nature of training and also provide a central organization which would enable local authorities to pool the cost. At present the smaller, poorer authorities, and those in remote areas, find it difficult or impossible to provide adequate facilities for young officers who wish to obtain qualifications; in these circumstances such authorities cannot recruit young people with legitimate ambitions. To pool the cost of training on a national basis will help the poorer authorities and thus ease the problem. The associations of local authorities accepted this recommendation immediately. The Local Government Training Board is now established and also incorporates the work of the Local Government Examinations Board.

One of the Mallaby recommendations is undeniably controversial – that local authorities should provide a career structure for lay administrative officers which would take them up to the second- or third-tier position in a local authority department. The use of the term 'lay administrative officer' is curious and potentially misleading; in normal usage, a 'lay' member of a local authority is thought to be an elected representative. The Mallaby Committee thought of a 'lay' officer as one who had not obtained a specialized professional qualification but who, instead, had obtained a broad education at a university or had studied for the Diploma in Municipal Administration. There is a clear analogy here with the general administrators who occupy the most senior posts in the Civil Service.

This proposal raises two issues. The first is the long-standing argument over the value of general education as opposed to specialized qualifications. Does a training confined to law, accountancy, engineering or medicine narrow the mind and so render men less able to carry out managerial functions? Is the man lacking specialized knowledge so much in the hands of specialists when dealing with practical problems as to be unable to provide effective leadership? The arguments are familiar. However, it is too often overlooked that the ability to administer, to make people work together as a team, to know when to use initiative and when to be cautious, to carry responsibility squarely but not too heavily – all these are functions of aptitude and personality, the development of which is perhaps but slightly affected by the subjects a person studies. If our senior civil servants are excellent administrators, is this because of the nature of their academic studies at Oxbridge or because they gained great benefit from the Oxbridge environment in their formative years? Leaving these general considerations on one side, it is true that if local government could provide an attractive career structure for those without the standard professional qualifications, then a wider range of persons might enter the local government service. University graduates in arts and social sciences may well be deterred from local government by the need to pass further examinations. But would the best graduates be attracted under the Mallaby proposal? They could expect only to get to the second or third post in a department and, in all normal circumstances, would be denied the top of the tree. Equally, if local authorities are reduced in number and increased in size, and if there is a tendency for local authority departments to be amalgamated, the number of chief officers will be drastically reduced in future and the status of the second or third ranking official would be greatly enhanced. So the 'lay administrative officer' scheme might prove to be reasonably popular with some potential recruits to local government. But the second objection to the proposal is that it could well be a disincentive to those thinking of obtaining advancement in local government through the normal professional channels because it would necessarily reduce the number of relatively senior and well-paid posts available to them. From the viewpoint of attracting able young men to local government the lay administrative officer scheme has the appearance of a two-edged sword.

It is for the individual local authority to decide upon the experience and qualifications of their middle-ranking officers. Thus establishment policies will vary. Certainly there is no rush of enthusiasm for the idea of lay administrative officers. This may be because of the strength of existing professional interests and traditions. Local authorities also feel that officers with professional qualifications are of greater *use* since they alone can carry out or supervise many of the practical tasks which form the core of local government activity. To some extent professional qualifications are indispensable; general administrators are not.

How far the Mallaby proposals, even if all carried out, would solve staffing problems is a matter for doubt. However, they cannot be considered in isolation. If the Maud Committee recommendations for drastic change in the internal structure of local authorities (considered in the following section) are implemented and succeed in improving the image of local government, this would do much to provide the local government service with a flow of able and vigorous recruits.

### CO-ORDINATION OF ADMINISTRATION AND POLICY

In districts and non-county boroughs there are usually four major departments, the Clerk's, the Treasurer's, the Engineer and Surveyor's and Public Health. There will be further departments if the authority runs trading services, exercises powers delegated by the county or has its own library. And as always in our local government system there are multifarious variations; some authorities have a separate Housing Department, a separate Architect's Department and so on. In top-tier authorities the total of departments is necessarily greater and will average about fifteen, although one Council has as many as thirty-five. The larger the number of departments, the greater is the need for co-ordination between their activities: the larger each single department, the greater is the need for co-ordination within it. There is a strong case for integrating together departments with allied responsibilities, so that officers with allied specialisms can more easily be welded into a united team and so reduce the possibility of inter-departmental rivalry and friction. The need for typing and clerical staff can usually be met more economically and effectively in a larger department. However, to arrange amalgamations is not easy. Officers with a particular brand of professional qualifications like to establish their own independent empires. The case for combining Health and Welfare Departments, in particular, is very strong but difficult to achieve.

Granted the crying need for co-ordination – how is it to be achieved? The standard answer is through the Clerk of the Council. A succession of official reports have urged this solution in varying terms. The Royal Commission on Local Government recommended in 1929 that the Clerk was the most suitable officer to achieve co-ordination and suggested that his ability to perform this task would depend on his personality. It did not propose that the Clerk be put in a position to give instructions to other chief officers. In 1934 the Hadow Committee on the Recruitment, Training and Promotion of Local Government Officers thought that the essential qualification of a Clerk was administrative ability. This view naturally opens up the argument whether a Clerk should necessarily have legal qualifications. The Treasury O and M Report on Coventry in 1953 again laid heavy emphasis on the administrative role of the Clerk; he should give continual consideration to measures which would achieve economies and be responsible for establishment work and an organization and methods service. This type of recommendation involves a very real difficulty. If the Clerk is to have an overall responsibility for the effective operation of all his council's activities, then he must be put in a position of seniority over other chief officers so that he is able, when necessary, to insist that they accept measures he feels requisite to secure economies. Naturally this involves some down-grading, some loss of independence, by other heads of departments and some change in the traditional practice that a chief officer is responsible to the council through his committee. Yet unless there is some loss of departmental independence there can be no guarantee that a local authority's administration is an effective unity.

The relationship between the Clerk and other principal officers is generally governed by ill-defined local conventions. A number of councils have taken steps to elevate the status of the Clerk by giving him some additional title such as 'Chief Administrative Officer'. Still in most authorities the pattern is determined by the interplay of personalities. When a new Clerk has to be appointed by a major authority, however, certain basic issues have to be faced. How wide shall the Clerk's administrative responsibilities be? How closely should they be defined? If emphasis is to be placed on his managerial function, need he necessarily be a lawyer or, indeed, have local government experience? And should the Clerk also be expected to advise the council on methods of policy co-ordination? The Maud Committee on Management of Local Government, leaning on the experience of foreign countries and of experiments at home at Newcastle and elsewhere, have stressed more firmly than earlier official reports that the Clerk should be the undisputed head of the council's staff. Since the legal profession is not a unique source of leadership ability and managerial acumen, it accepted also that the Clerk need not be a lawyer.

Developments at Newcastle are certainly worthy of attention. The retirement of the Town Clerk in 1965 provided an opportunity for the City Council to carry through a drastic modification to its internal structure. It decided to appoint a 'city manager' who would be in full charge of City administration: the actual title 'city manager' was not used owing to its American overtones. The man chosen for the post, Mr Frank Harris, was previously an executive of the Ford Motor Company, and was paid a salary in excess of that normally paid to Town Clerks: if local government wants to recruit big business executives it must pay business-style salaries. Mr Harris subsequently proposed a drastic simplification of the City's committee structure. The number of committees was to be reduced from thirty-seven to eight, two of which were to have novel functions – one responsible for 'Municipal Relations' and the other for 'Resources Planning'. Municipal Relations was taken to include relations between the council and its employees, the public and Parliament, the control of manpower and pay, communications within the organization and the allocation of responsibility and authority. The Resources Planning Committee was to be a key policy committee surveying the allocation of resources between the various facilities and services provided by the municipality and be concerned with environmental planning in the widest sense. It had some similarity to the management board subsequently proposed by Maud. The Municipal Relations and Resources Planning committees were intended to be superior to other council committees. This down-grading of other committees was a main reason why the scheme proved unacceptable to the Labour majority and so was not adopted. However, in 1967 a major reorganization was carried through which reduced the number of committees and sub-committees by two-thirds. The work-load of elected members was cut by nearly a half and a greater proportion of committee time was used for discussion of policy. At Newcastle two bodies play a key role in the co-ordination of policy, the Finance Committee and the Leader's Conference; the latter is a recent development which permits leading members of the majority party to discuss major policy issues with officers, often before they reach committees, in an unpolitical atmosphere free from press reporters.

The upheavals at Newcastle have two aspects. One is the nature of the top appointment; the other is the streamlining of council business. They raise quite separate issues. On the personal aspect, if other major authorities were to follow Newcastle's lead, then promotion prospects for Clerks and their deputies would be severely cut. And it is also a matter for argument whether the chief executive of a local authority ought to have local government experience. A large local authority is big business in the sense of the scale of its undertakings and the amount of its financial turnover, but it has not got a profit-making ethos and the nature of its relations with the public must differ from those of a commercial firm. While the Newcastle type of appointment is no longer unique, witness the Greater London Council, the example has not been widely followed.

Other authorities have made changes designed to assist policy co-ordination. Developments at West Bromwich have been very different from those at Newcastle. Instead of simply elevating the status of the Town Clerk, six chief officers have been appointed as co-ordinators: the Town Clerk in relation to central administration and legal matters; the Borough Treasurer for finance; the Medical Officer of Health for social services; the Director of Education for educational and cultural activities; the Borough Surveyor for engineering and civic services; the Transport Manager for transport services. An obvious difficulty about this scheme is the determination of boundaries between these officers. Is refuse collection essentially engineering or transport? Are ambulances transport or a social service? And as there are so many co-ordinators, can they themselves be co-ordinated effectively? Can the professional independence of other chief officers be sufficiently safeguarded? Nevertheless, the scheme has attractions in that similar services can be brought to work more closely together than by simply nominating the Town Clerk as an overlord. The West Bromwich changes were affected at the same time as its area was extended following the report of the Boundary Commission: this suggests that geographical reform can be a useful stimulus to administrative reform. The West Bromwich committee system was also streamlined – always a delicate task because fewer committees mean fewer committee chairmanships.

Not only boroughs have felt the need for a shake-up. Basildon U.D.C. and Cheshire are just two more examples of authorities who have engaged in self enquiry. Basildon has created an Executive Committee to stand between the council and other committees to co-ordinate policy. Where a council is dominated by party politics, the majority party may agree that a group of its leaders form a local 'cabinet' to exercise a general oversight of business. This device suffers from the disadvantage that party gatherings are unofficial and therefore the officers of the local authority cannot be present to give advice. However, in a few authorities this 'cabinet' has been accepted as a council committee and thus is entitled to the full assistance of the permanent staff. Incidentally, such an arrangement was operating in Newcastle before 1965. But even where this mechanism has evolved to facilitate policy leadership, not enough has been done to rationalize committee work or to meet the criticisms made at the end of the previous chapter.

The Maud Committee produced a comprehensive plan in 1967 to ensure co-ordination of both administration and policy in local authorities. This involved a drastic reappraisal of the nature of committee work and the structure of local administration. A diagram illustrating the essence of the Maud proposals is given below. The core of this scheme was that each council should appoint a 'management board' consisting of between five and nine members of the council. The management board would formulate major policies and present them for approval to the council; it would have overall

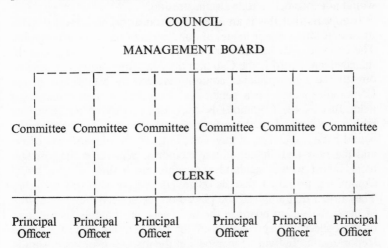

COUNCIL

MANAGEMENT BOARD

Committee Committee Committee Committee Committee Committee

CLERK

Principal Officer   Principal Officer   Principal Officer   Principal Officer   Principal Officer   Principal Officer

responsibility for the execution of these policies; it would take decisions on matters which exceeded the authority of chief officers; it would recommend proposals to the council on items which exceeded its own delegated powers. The Clerk would be responsible to the management board and through it to the council; he would also be the undisputed head of the whole of the staff. The heads of departments would be answerable to the Clerk and *not* to any committee. Obviously this plan provides unity and centralization of decision-making achieved by down-grading all principal officers other than the Clerk and by down-grading all committees in relation to the management board. Thus in the diagram the unbroken lines indicate chains of command and the broken lines are channels of advice. The Maud Committee is specific about the new role of committees: 'Committees should not be directing or controlling bodies nor should they be concerned with routine administration'. What then are the committees to do? They would make recommendations to the management board on 'major objectives' and study how these could best be carried out. They would review progress in the sphere of the particular service that concerned them, consider reactions of the public and deal with any matters referred to them by the management board. Executive decisions would only be made in exceptional circumstances and when the management board required this to be done: the implication is that delegated authority would normally be given to officers rather than committees. The scheme also permits a committee to consider any matter raised by its own members, but this seems to conflict with the principle noted above that committees would not consider routine administration.

It appears that this is an attempt to transform each local government unit into a minor model of our system of national government. The council is Parliament, or perhaps the House of Commons; the management board is the Cabinet; the committees are to be analogous to the new specialist committees recently established in the Commons to exercise a general advisory function in a particular field. Just as the Commons is composed largely of backbenchers with a lesser number of Government ministers, so local authorities would have two classes of members, those on the management board and the rank-and-file committee members. Service on the management board would inevitably consume much time, so the Maud Committee proposed that its members receive part-time salaries They urged that emphasis be placed on the collective responsibility of the management board in the same way, presumably, as we think of the collective responsibility of the Cabinet. To quote the Maud Report again, 'Individual members of the management board should have special spheres of interest and speak on them': this appears to mean that one member would become the local Chancellor of the Exchequer, another the local Minister of Education, another the local Minister of Transport and so on. Committee meetings would normally be open to the press: meetings of the management board would be private: most committee meetings in the Commons are public, but Cabinet meetings are not! The parallels are remarkably close.

It is not surprising that this Report has aroused much criticism, a lot of which is defensive and comes from those who wish to retain established positions. And before reviewing the objections one should also stress that they are themselves a tribute to the quality of the Report. If a scheme contains little that is new, if its proposals can easily be condemned, then it merits a minimum of attention. Because the Maud Report raises fundamental issues about our local government institutions and illuminates serious shortcomings in their practical operation, it has stimulated a great debate.

To force local government to move towards our system of national government is to introduce the deficiencies of parliament into local government. Thus M.P.s have insufficient information to act as a check on government departments. Under the Maud plan will councillors have enough information to be able to challenge the management board? The Maud scheme calls for fewer committees and a maximum committee membership of fifteen to include co-opted members: this implies that the back-bench councillor would sit on one, or at the most two committees. Would not the backbench councillor know less of the operations of his authority than at present? Certainly he will be separated from financial administration. In this situation could a council be expected to scrutinize effectively the decisions of its management board? Another inevitable shortcoming of the House of Commons is that the scale of representation is low. On average an M.P. is expected to serve 80,000 people. In local government the proportion of representatives is much higher; but with bigger authorities, smaller councils and smaller committees this would change for the worse – perhaps dramatically so.

Possibly the gravest criticism is contained in the Report itself in a note of dissent by one of the members of the Maud Committee, Sir Andrew Wheatley. While accepting the concept of the management board, Sir Andrew argued that committees must be given wider scope than that allowed to them in the Committee's plan. He feared that the management board might become too autocratic and remote from other members of a council and that this would damage the essential democratic quality of our local government. He also argued that if backbench members of a local council were limited to a minor advisory role there would not be a sufficient incentive for able people to come forward and offer themselves as candidates at local elections. To serve on a committee without executive responsibilities is a sure prescription for frustration. As an alternative, therefore, Sir Andrew proposed that committees be given some executive powers, and while they should always consult with the management board they should, in case of disagreement, report direct to the council. This view has much to commend it but such disagreement would be highly unlikely in any authority run on strict party lines: it is relevant also that party influence is increasing steadily and will become more pronounced if local authorities become fewer and larger.

The Maud Committee gave very full consideration to the impact of party politics in local government. On one matter they wished to depart from the national government model because they argue that minority parties should be represented on the management board. The Leader of the Opposition is not a member of the Cabinet! However, a strong case can be made for this arrangement. Ideally, members of all parties should be able to contribute to the good management of public affairs. Much of local administration is, or ought to be, essentially non-political in character. And unless minority supporters have an opportunity to serve on the management board, there will be a break in continuity and a lack of experience whenever the party majority on the council changes. Even so, it is difficult to see how a local political 'cabinet' can effectively discuss controversial matters if their leading opponents are always present. There is no suggestion that the management board should be a 'coalition government'. Minority representation also implies that the management board as a whole would not be responsible for the conduct of affairs but solely those members who belong to the local majority party. Further, many authorities remain non-political. Could the Maud plan work if the management board were not sustained by party discipline? Without such restraints is there not a likelihood of conflict? If the backbench members of councils are independent in attitude and action, then they may vote the management board out of office, especially as the salaries of board members would become available for redistribution. The management board cannot appeal to the electors against the council – as a Prime Minister and his Cabinet can dissolve Parliament – because local elections are still to be held on fixed dates. Should not dismissal of the board require a local general election?

Other aspects of the Maud Report are considered in the final chapter of this book. The intention here has been to summarize those proposals concerned with the internal administration of local authorities. Critics can urge that instead of producing ideas designed to attract people to local government – as instructed by its terms of reference – the Maud plan may repel potential councillors. Faced with the choice between democracy and efficiency, it can be argued that the Report leaned too far towards efficiency, that its contribution to efficiency is also in doubt since it opens up new possibilities of local autocracy and unfeeling bureaucracy. The contrary argument is that our concept of democracy in local government must be adjusted to modern conditions. These issues are of basic importance and permit no simple clear-cut solutions.

Meanwhile, what are the prospects of action? Some legal changes are required before the Maud scheme could be put into force, relating *inter alia* to the appointment of officers, the appointment of committees, and the ability to delegate authority. There will also be a tendency to delay reforms until a new geographical structure of local government has been worked out, i.e. until the Royal Commission on Local Government has reported and until a new pattern of local authorities becomes a reality. Indeed, the Maud style reforms are not suitable for the smaller second-tier units that exist today.

## MODERN TECHNIQUES OF MANAGEMENT

There is a third broad aspect of the quest for efficiency in local government consisting of various techniques that have been developed to promote the efficiency of office and outdoor staff. They all involve investigation combined with some element of numerical analysis. Processes of this type may also be used to organize information in a way which will help decision making. The following paragraphs give an outline description of these methods, their uses and their limitations.

The concept of work-study originated in industry. It is concerned with the examination of productive processes to improve efficiency, and developed a number of aspects including the design of machines and equipment, the layout of working areas, and the pattern of labour organization. The introduction of any bonus incentive payment usually involves some element of work measurement in order to define a norm that must be exceeded if additional payment is to be made; such measurement is another function of the work-study expert. Organization and methods work is rather more recent in origin and developed in the Civil Service during the last war in response to the need to save manpower and limit administrative expenditure. It concentrated on the use of office machines, the design and simplification of forms and, in general, re-examined the need for traditional administrative practices. It also looked into the distribution of functions between Government departments. O and M work, as it is popularly called, has thus a similar purpose to work-study, and the distinction between the two is increasingly blurred.

In local government interest in O and M activity developed in the nineteen-fifties. Elected members of local authorities welcomed it as a possible means of cutting expenditure fairly painlessly and so reducing the demand on the ratepayer. Some of the younger and more ambitious local government officers saw O and M as providing a new and stimulating career opportunity. Many of the larger authorities have appointed their own O and M officers and the former Metropolitan Boroughs combined to establish a joint O and M unit. Elsewhere local authorities called in the services of business efficiency consultants, who normally are engaged by private firms to advise how their organization and profitability could be improved. The use of consultants in local government did not always have happy results. Since their fees were high it was apparent that money would be wasted, not saved, unless their reports showed the way to significant economies. Other difficulties were caused because sometimes they were unfamiliar with local government law, traditions and practice. And whether or not business consultants are used for this work, it is generally true that there has been more resistance in local government to O and M activity than in the Civil Service. This is not surprising. The Civil Service is such a vast organization that it is unlikely that any single O and M report will significantly affect career prospects of established staff and any redundancies can be smoothed over by moving people on to other duties or by dismissing temporary staff. Local authorities, being much smaller administrative units, do not provide such good opportunities for redeployment of staff. But resistance to O and M activity arises for other reasons. A crucial issue is how far-reaching should an O and M investigation be? Should it be limited to the pattern of office processes – or should it extend to the committee structure of an authority, to the division of responsibility between departments of a local authority, to the relations between committees and officers and, in particular, to how far decisions should be delegated by elected representatives to paid officials? These are fundamental questions which some councillors and some officials would prefer to avoid. Yet any management survey is emasculated if a local authority regards its *modus operandi* as being beyond reproach. Just occasionally friction has also arisen over the question of how much publicity should be given to O and M reports. Some councillors and aldermen put the argument like this: if public money is spent to enquire into the efficiency of our authority, then the public are entitled to know the full results of the enquiry. But it is generally accepted that establishment matters, as they affect individuals, should remain confidential. Of course, should an O and M report suggest a basic reorganization of departments or a re-shaping of committees, then some public discussion must take place.

Operational research involves the study of routine tasks by specialists skilled in scientific observations who are usually expert statisticians. The idea is that an essentially mathematical investigation can provide valuable information that will act as a guide towards making the best possible decisions. A few examples will help to demonstrate the kind of problems that can be submitted to this type of examination. Invoices are normally checked to ensure that they are correct both in terms of arithmetic and as a record of goods received. But checking invoices costs money. How far would it be economical in any office to save the cost of checking and bear the risk of loss through inaccuracies going undetected? In any store, whether of materials needed in construction or in a store of office materials, the problem arises of how large an order to place for any item in regular demand. Infrequent ordering of large quantities saves time and trouble and may offer discounts for purchase in bulk, but large stocks demand larger storage space and involve spending money before it is absolutely necessary. What point on the scale between infrequent big orders and many small orders will give the best results? A proportion of outside staff employed on refuse collection is always absent from work for sickness or other reasons; if a refuse collection service is to be constantly regular some surplus labour will have to be employed to make up for the absentees. How much surplus labour is necessary to give a guarantee of regular collection? These are the type of questions to which operational research is applied. It is not possible, of course, within the confines of a short book on local government to explain the mathematical techniques which are used in the solution of problems.

This sort of research is not an infallible magic that can always lead the way to the best possible decision. Major decisions usually involve value judgments which may be of a political nature or simply raise the issue of how much people are prepared to pay to achieve a certain quality of service. Let us revert to the example of refuse collection. A piece of operational research might show that if 20 per cent more dustmen are employed above the number required if all men were always on duty, then the chances of maintaining regular collection are about 99 per cent. But a council might well take the view that they were prepared to face a higher risk of irregular collection rather than bear the cost of the additional labour involved. Or to revert to the case of invoice checking, a council might not be willing to reduce standards of internal auditing because of the visitations of the District Auditor. But operational research can provide a firm basis of information on which decisions can be made. Without such impersonal investigations, decisions on administrative methods will be made on the basis of hopes, hunches or traditions, i.e. a problem is dealt with in a particular way because it was handled like that in the past when, quite possibly, conditions of scale or cost were quite different.

Cost-benefit analysis is another technique that has been developed to aid decision-making. This is more usually applied to projected future capital developments. If there are alternative schemes for highway development, the more expensive providing for freer, faster and perhaps safer traffic flow, which should be chosen? The idea of cost-benefit analysis, put simply, is to estimate the costs and benefits of alternative plans and to demonstrate their relative advantages. Here again there are substantial difficulties. Any estimate of future benefit must be hypothetical to some degree. Some benefits cannot be quantified or translated into monetary terms, e.g. a design for a road or a building may be aesthetically more pleasing than a cheaper design, but one cannot make a scientific estimate of the benefit to be derived from beauty. And when an analysis is completed there remains the basic value judgment of how much we are prepared to contribute now to benefit the next generation. This can be illustrated again in terms of highway development. Given certain expectations of the growth of motor traffic, a relatively modest scheme of highway improvement may be thought adequate to meet the needs of the next decade while a more elaborate scheme would be adequate for a much longer period. Which scheme should be adopted? Cost-benefit analysis cannot answer this problem. It can provide material upon which a more informed judgment can be made in that people can be made aware of the probable consequences of any decision.

This new emphasis on research and quantification as a preliminary to the taking of decisions has increased the need to carry out complex calculations with speed and accuracy. The growth of local authority administration also demands that routine office work be mechanized as far as possible. Together these requirements have produced a rapid increase in the use of computers in local government; many large councils have installed their own machines and often arrange to share their use with neighbouring authorities. A computer is a highly sophisticated piece of electronic technology. Only a limited number of specialists understand fully how they work. But it will be necessary for an increasing number of administrators to know what computers can do to help their work and, indeed, to know how to give instructions to the machines. Hence the very great interest in systems analysis and computer programming. Applications of the new technology are developing steadily, some of their most common uses are for regular payments of all kinds, e.g. wages and interest charges, the preparation of election registers and data storage and analysis of expenditure and income, of costing, of statistics relating to planning applications, traffic flows, health records and education.

*Chapter VIII*

---

# THE REORGANIZATION OF STRUCTURE

### THE CHALLENGE OF RIVAL INSTITUTIONS

For a century after the reform of the poor law in 1834 local authorities enjoyed a steady growth of their responsibilities. The scale of their duties reached its apogee in 1939. Since then a number of functions have been handed over to other bodies. Local authority hospitals were transferred in 1948 to bodies nominated by the Minister of Health. At the same period municipal gas and electricity undertakings were absorbed by public corporations; the Inland Revenue were entrusted with valuation for local rating purposes, and the National Assistance Board was established to relieve poverty. The loss of further powers, notably ambulance and passenger transport undertakings, is a distinct possibility.

How can this change of fortune be explained? There were two main reasons for the burgeoning of local government after 1834. The agreement that public provision of services should be allowed to develop was a hesitant agreement, for this period was the heyday of individualistic doctrines. The sentiment that government of any kind is but a necessary evil leads also to the supposition that local government is a lesser evil than national government because it is more susceptible to public control. The great indignation aroused by the attempts of the national government to influence local affairs in the Chadwick period is eloquent proof of the force of this attitude. The second reason can be stated quite simply – local government had no competitors. The highly competent Civil Service of today evolved very slowly in the latter part of the nineteenth century. Even in the early years of this century the organizational resources of government departments were rudimentary except for tax collection. Public corporations did not appear until the nineteen-twenties. Thus the administrative capacity of local authorities, however deficient it may have been by modern standards, held a dominating position.

All this has now changed. Collectivism is in fashion rather than individualism: technical requirements demand large scale production to achieve economies of scale: the need for efficiency and uniformity is held to require fewer and bigger units of organization. Thus local government is on the defensive. In any discussion about how a new service should be provided, or how some existing service could be reformed, the case for local government no longer dominates; on the contrary, it is far more difficult to sustain. Besides the challenge from government departments, public corporations and *ad hoc* boards, a new competitor to local authorities is threatening to emerge in the form of regionalism. What form this threat may take depends on the future pattern of regional institutions. This is not easy to foresee because the concept of regionalism has developed in recent years from quite separate pressures and has aroused different reactions as between the political parties. In Wales the idea has been pushed forward by advocates of Welsh Nationalism. The need to develop the less prosperous areas of the country where unemployment is highest has enhanced regional consciousness and led to demands for action on a regional scale, particularly in Wales, North-east and South-west England. In the over-crowded South-east of the country there has been growing recognition that the problems of housing, town development and road traffic demand some type of planning control which covers a wider area than the existing local planning authorities – the county councils and the county boroughs.

Before the 1964 General Election the three political parties each adopted a distinctive attitude towards these issues. Liberals urged the creation of popularly elected regional authorities. Labour linked the idea of regionalism with the need for national economic planning under a new Ministry of Economic Affairs; under this new department regional planning boards would be formed which would work closely with representatives of local government and both sides of industry. Thus local authorities would nominate people to advise the regional staff of central government. The Conservatives argued that the necessary planning and co-ordination could be achieved simply by the development of the regional activities of existing government departments; they opposed the creation of regional councils, either elected or nominated, on the grounds that such councils could not eliminate the clash of interest within a region, that in some areas a regional consciousness had scarcely developed and that major decisions always had to be taken by the Government which alone could view the national situation as a whole. It is true that within a region there will always be conflicting opinions. Separate areas will put in competing claims for development of industry and communications. The interests of agriculture and tourism will not coincide with those of heavy industry and mining. But merely because differences of this nature are inevitable does not imply, surely, that there is no need for formal machinery of consultation.

After the Labour Party had won the 1964 General Election, regional planning machinery of the type the Party had advocated was duly created. Scotland and Wales were treated as separate regions. Initially, in England six regions were created.

1. Northern, including Cumberland, Durham, Northumberland, Westmorland and Yorkshire (North Riding): Headquarters Newcastle.
2. North West, including Cheshire, Lancashire and the High Peak area: Headquarters Manchester.
3. Yorkshire and Humberside, including Lincolnshire (Lindsey) and Yorkshire (East and West Riding): Headquarters Leeds.
4. East Midlands, including Derbyshire, Leicestershire, Lincolnshire (Holland and Kesteven), Northamptonshire, Nottinghamshire and Rutland: Headquarters Nottingham.
5. West Midlands, including Herefordshire, Shropshire, Staffordshire, Warwickshire and Worcestershire: Headquarters Birmingham.
6. South West, including Cornwall, Devon, Dorset, Gloucestershire, Somerset and Wiltshire: Headquarters Bristol.

Subsequently two further regions were formed covering the Southeast of the country.

7. East Anglia, including Norfolk, Suffolk, Cambridgeshire and Huntingdon and Peterborough: Headquarters London.
8. South East England, covering the remainder of the country: Headquarters London.

Each region has an Economic Planning Board consisting of civil servants representing the various ministries concerned with economic and physical planning and an advisory Economic Planning Council consisting of representatives of various interests within each region – including, of course, local government. Inevitably, a number of difficulties attended the birth of these new organizations. There were geographical problems. Sheffield felt that it should have been the centre of a separate region. Perhaps with more justice Devon and Cornwall claimed separate treatment; the distance from Lands End to the north of Gloucestershire is roughly 250 miles. Then there were problems of representation. Not all the major authorities, county councils and county boroughs, could be given a place on the Planning Councils and those left out felt some resentment. But this arrangement has the advantage that local authority representatives do not think of themselves as delegates to the Planning Council from their own area: as not all areas are represented then it is obviously necessary for the local government nominees to try to advance the interests of the region as a whole. But the major objections came from many people in the world of local government who thought that the new regional bodies would reduce the status and powers of local authorities. It was argued that bureaucratic government at regional level would leave less and less responsibility for local authorities. If the planning, housing and highway work of local government was to be supervised in regional offices, it was feared that local authorities would lose the right of access to Whitehall. And if decisions were to be made in the regional capitals rather than Whitehall it seemed possible that Members of Parliament would be less able to influence or even speed up these decisions. Perhaps because the Government had such a small majority in 1965 it took some pains to abate these worries and reassure local authorities. The original names 'regional planning boards', 'regional planning councils' were changed to *economic* planning boards and councils to place the stress on industrial development. It was emphasized that the new bodies would in no sense supercede local authorities or take over any of their existing functions.

It is too early to make a final judgment on our new regional institutions. As yet their impact has been unimpressive. The fears expressed at their inception have so far appeared groundless. But the economic climate since 1965 has not been conducive to the planning and implementation of spectacular plans for development. The Planning Councils, as advisory bodies, have no executive authority. With an occasional exception, their work attracts little publicity and enjoys little support and understanding. It is often argued that unless regional councils are elected they will attract no public interest and their advice will carry little weight with Ministers.

However, this regional planning machinery does not stand alone. In recent years various other regional institutions have evolved; more are in prospect. They cover diverse subjects, e.g. sports facilities, further education, the arts and passenger transport. All have some impact on the work of local authorities. All may be affected by the reconstruction of local government. Alternatively, the reshaping of local authorities may itself be influenced by the existence of regional institutions. It is too early to see. But the growth of regionalism in the nineteen-sixties is a major factor in the developing situation and is further evidence of the recognition of the need for wider administrative areas.

## THE NEED FOR REFORM

Our present structure of local government was fashioned at the end of the nineteenth century by three Acts of Parliament which constituted a noble embodiment of the reforming democratic spirit of late-Victorian England. In geographical terms they commonly utilized boundaries which already existed, including county boundaries which can be traced back to feudal times. The present structure was, therefore, created in a different age for the needs of a different age, when the duties of local authorities were far more limited than they are today and when the internal combustion engine had not revolutionized means of transport. The twentieth century has done little so far to modernize the Victorian legacy. True there have been some changes. Between 1888 and 1929 just over twenty new county boroughs were created; in the nineteen-thirties the number of county districts was substantially reduced; boundaries of boroughs have widened to embrace advancing suburbia; some urban districts have achieved the dignity of borough status and so have become able to parade a Mayor and aldermen on ceremonial occasions. But the pace of change has been slowed down by the clash of local interests, particularly between counties and boroughs. The counties managed to prevent the establishment of any new county boroughs between 1929 and 1964, motivated by the fear that new county boroughs would mean loss of some rateable value.

Thus the local government map has failed to adjust to movements and growth of population. Anomalies inherited from the Victorians have become more glaring while others have emerged. The largest administrative county, Lancashire, has a population of over one hundred times greater than that of Radnor and over eighty times greater than that of Rutland. In the county borough class, Birmingham is thirty times the size of Canterbury. There are also second-tier authorities with a population three times that of Canterbury. Over thirty county districts, most of them in Wales, have less than 2,000 inhabitants. It is even possible to find third-tier authorities, suburbanized parishes in rural districts, with a population not far short of that of Radnor.

The existence of many small county districts has had a profound effect on the allocation of local government duties. Recent legislation has assumed, with minor exceptions, e.g. libraries, that all local authorities of any one type must be given equal statutory rights in respect of any function. It has also been held that functions cannot be sub-divided, so that if a county must be given a particular part of a function, like education, it must have the whole of it. Again, highways are a notable exception to this rule. But the total effect has been to drain functions away from the second-tier authorities and to change the pattern of local administration not by a comprehensive scheme of reform but by *ad hoc* measures relating to individual functions. Thus the second-tier authorities have lost powers over elementary education, planning, fire service, personal health services and rural roads to the county councils. This aggravated tensions between counties and the larger county districts and led to demands for the delegation of county responsibilities to the larger districts – a clumsy compromise that often worked badly.

Another out-dated concept that still remains is the differentiation between urban and rural areas. The nineteenth century legislation was based on the belief that the countryside needed fewer services than the towns, notably in relation to sewerage. This view is no longer acceptable. The difference in powers between urban and rural districts is now small but twin organizations with virtually identical tasks are often located in the same small town where the urban district or borough serves an inner area and is divided by an antique boundary from the rural district serving the hinterland. At the top-tier level the same duplication can arise between county council and county borough with more serious results. Ultimately at national level the urban-rural differentiation has produced the conflict between the County Councils Association and the Association of Municipal Corporations that has done much to inhibit basic structural reform.

The main failing of the present system, however, is that many of the top-tier units are too small. Specialized services which demand the use of highly qualified staff, purpose-built accommodation and expensive equipment can only be provided economically for a substantial population. Planning also cannot be carried out effectively except over wide areas. Exactly how big the top-tier units should be is a matter of constant argument, but estimates of size continually increase. In 1888 the minimum population for county borough status was 50,000 and four exceptions below that figure were permitted. In 1926 the minimum was raised to 75,000; in 1958 to 100,000. Evidence given by government departments to the present Royal Commission thinks in terms of 200,000–300,000 while the County Councils Association talks of half a million. Government departments are attracted by the idea of fewer and larger local authorities as being easier to supervise in the interests of uniformity. Local authorities increasingly accept the need for bigger units out of fear that they will lose functions to other sectors of public administration.

LACK OF PROGRESS 1945–66

During the last war, considerable interest developed in the need for local government reform. In part, this was an aspect of the nation-wide discussion on post-war reconstruction, in part it was stimulated because the existing structure of authorities was seen to be ill-adapted to meet the emergencies of war. Various plans were put forward, e.g. by the Labour Party, the Association of Municipal Corporations and NALGO, each of which recognized the need for larger areas of administration for some purposes. These reports now belong to the history of local government but they helped to create a climate of opinion which caused the Government to take action.

Almost the last measure of the war-time coalition Cabinet was to promote the Local Government (Boundary Commission) Act, 1945, which established a Boundary Commission authorized to propose limited changes outside London. The limitations were all important, for the Commission was given no power over functions, so it could not introduce any new *type* of authority. Any prospect of regional government was eliminated from the start. (Local authorities were very hostile to the regional concept because of their dealings with the war-time Regional Commissioners.) Also excluded was any new arrangement to deal with the special problems of conurbations. The Commission had to work within the traditional model of local gov-ernment: it could divide and amalgamate counties, demote county boroughs, create new ones, or amalgamate and divide them, and change the geographical arrangement of second-tier authorities. The Commission studied their problem for over two years, then reported that their powers were insufficient to initiate the changes needed and set out the details of a wholly new structure. One-tier local govern-ment was to be kept in only seventeen of the largest cities with a mini-mum population of 200,000, to be known as one-tier counties. The remainder of the country, including the Lancashire-Cheshire conur-bations, was to have a two-tier system. The major authorities would be reshaped counties, again with a minimum population of 200,000, so that the smaller counties would be amalgamated and in a few cases the largest counties would be sub-divided. Within these coun-ties would be boroughs and urban and rural districts, together with a new type of authority confusingly termed 'county boroughs' which would exercise all powers except for planning, police, fire service and main roads. The new county boroughs would be Liverpool, Manchester and other towns in the population bracket 60,000–200,000. Thus there were to be three categories of town, one-tier counties, county boroughs and other boroughs: this plan had the advantage of easing the sharp contrast in status between county boroughs of the existing type and other urban authorities, a contrast which has grown steadily greater during this century.

The changes proposed were far too sweeping to be easily acceptable, although they were the minimum demanded by the situation. In 1949 the Boundary Commission was dissolved and its ideas were consigned unloved to Civil Service archives.

The issue then remained dormant until 1953 when the Conservative Government asked the associations of local authorities to re-examine the issues. It seemed that the Government hoped that the associations might arrive at an agreed set of principles that could provide the basis for reform. The hope was delusory. The Association of Municipal Corporations produced a scheme favouring one-tier all-purpose authorities – county boroughs wherever possible. The other four associations, the County Councils Association, Urban District Councils Association, Rural District Councils Association and the National Association of Parish Councils argued the advantages of the existing pattern or two- and three-tier local administration and urged that county boroughs be made to conform to it. The Government then indicated that it would not agree to enter two-tier administration in the counties or single-tier administration in the largest towns. Subsequently, the associations all accepted that a new boundary commission be established with an understanding that the normal population qualification for county borough status would be 100,000, or 125,000 in the conurbations. There was also a general acceptance of the need to examine whether further powers could be delegated by counties to districts with a population over 60,000. Delegation was the sop offered by counties to the larger districts deprived of the opportunity of achieving county borough status.

The Local Government Act, 1958, thereupon established two fresh Boundary Commissions, one for England and one for Wales. These bodies were born as a result of an armistice between the clashing interests of counties and boroughs.

The Local Government Commissions were guided in their work by a set of Regulations issued by the Government under the authority of the Local Government Act, 1958. The Regulations instructed the Commissions to establish 'effective and convenient local government' and to pay attention to the following points when remodelling areas:

(a) community of interest;

(b) development and expected development;

(c) economic and industrial characteristics;

(d) financial resources measured in relation to financial need;

(e) physical features, including suitable boundaries, means of communication and accessibility to administrative centres and
centres of business and social life;

(f) population – size, distribution and characteristics;

(g) record of administration of the local authorities concerned;

(h) size and shape of the areas of local government;

(i) wishes of the inhabitants.

These items are not set out in order of importance: it will be noticed
that the order is alphabetical. Nor were these pointers exclusive, for
the Commissions could take other matters into account if they
wished so to do. A population of 100,000 was presumed to be adequate for the proper discharge of the duties of a county borough; a
smaller population would be regarded as sufficient only in special
circumstances.

As noted above, the Commissions were instructed to carry out
their tasks within the present framework of county and county
borough organization. Thus they could propose the creation or amalgamation and demotion of county boroughs; they could suggest
boundary adjustments between top-tier authorities. In the conurbations (described in the 1958 Act as the special review areas of Tyneside, West Yorkshire, South-east Lancashire, Merseyside and the
West Midlands) the English Commission did have wider powers,
for it could propose in these areas the establishment of a 'continuous
county' in which there would be no county boroughs and in which
the distribution of functions between the county and the second-tier
authorities might depart from the normal pattern. Also in the special
review areas the English Commission had to consider the boundaries
of the district and non-county borough councils.

The Local Government Commission for England divided the
country into areas and studied them piecemeal; the Welsh Commission dealt with its task as a whole. As a start, the Commissions held
preliminary consultations with local authorities and then issued
draft proposals. Before changes could take place, there was a long
road to travel. First, the local authorities concerned had a right to
lodge objections and to hold a formal conference with the Commission. The Commission then submitted their plans, with or without
modifications, to the Ministry of Housing and Local Government.
The Minister would then invite further comment and objections from
the local authorities and might arrange for a further public enquiry
to be held. Ultimately the Minister had to decide the issues in dispute
and place the Government view before Parliament in the form of an
Order which required parliamentary approval. After all this, once
any adjustments to its own boundaries had been settled, each county

had to review non-county boroughs, district councils and parishes: as usual, final decisions on any changes would be subject to Ministerial approval.

It follows that the reorganization of local authorities was a protracted business. Plenty of opportunity was given for public opinion to make itself felt; the force of opinion might cause a Commission to change its mind or lead the Minister to reject the final plans of a Commission. There was a tendency for each stage of decision-making to reduce the amount of change. This is well illustrated by developments in the East Midlands. Originally, the English Commission wished to amalgamate into a single administrative county the existing counties of Cambridgeshire, Isle of Ely, Huntingdonshire and the Soke of Peterborough, together with small parts of Rutland, Northamptonshire and Lincoln (Kesteven). The city of Cambridge was to become a county borough and the remainder of Rutland was to be incorporated with Leicestershire. These ideas caused a chorus of protest and criticism from local interests adversely affected; the resistance of Rutland attracted considerable national publicity. The final plan of the Commission showed major changes from their preliminary suggestions. Rutland was not to be divided but combined with Leicestershire as a whole. The Lincolnshire boundary was untouched. Most important of all, the proposed four-county amalgamation was dropped: instead the Soke of Peterborough was to join Huntingdonshire to make one new county, while the Isle of Ely would link with Cambridgeshire to make a second new county. The recommendation to make the City of Cambridge a county borough was withdrawn because without the support of the City the new county of Cambridge would be too weak to provide effective local administration. Naturally the City objected to the loss of the prospect of independence, especially as the Commission had accepted that it possessed adequate resources to become an efficient county borough. The Minister accepted the second plan with the important difference that Rutland was reprieved to continue as a separate county. This was, of course, a great victory for those people in Rutland who had campaigned so vigorously to retain their independence. It must have given encouragement to others elsewhere who objected to the Commission's ideas for their own locality.

In the West Midlands the main proposal of the Commission was to transform twenty-six authorities of various types into five new county boroughs. This plan was sternly contested and the councils concerned used every device available to frustrate reform. Wednesbury in association with other authorities initiated an action in the High Court seeking a declaration that the Minister's acceptance of the Commission's plan was invalid because the enquiry into objections against the plan had not been properly conducted. Wednesbury's case was that the inspector holding the enquiry had considered only the objections to the Commission's plan and not the merits of alternative schemes suggested by the objectors at the enquiry. The Courts rejected this claim, holding that the purpose of the enquiry was administrative rather than judicial and that there was no statutory requirement that it must consider alternative proposals to those of the Commission. All this took time as the authorities took their case to the Court of Appeal and were finally refused leave to appeal to the Lords by their Lordships' Appeal Committee. A similar case brought by Burton-on-Trent, who objected to losing county borough status, was also unsuccessful. Wednesbury continued its fight in the Upper House by invoking a little used procedure requiring the House, as a legislative body, to examine the Minister's Order designed to exterminate them. The procedure in the Upper House governing Statutory Instruments is complex. Put briefly, it was that any Order concerned with a Special Review Area or which affected a county or county borough could be the subject of a petition to the Special Orders Committee of the Lords which could, in turn, decide to refer the petition to a select committee. It is quite clear that these possibilities had been overlooked when the 1958 Local Government Act was drafted. Ultimately the Special Orders Committee rejected the Midlanders' petition and the Commission's plan was approved after debates in both Houses in December, 1965. This was a little more than four and a half years after the plan had first been submitted to the Minister. Even this delay might be regarded as tolerable were the final solution satisfactory. But does not the Black Country and the Birmingham area require a single top-tier authority to deal with such basic problems as planning and overspill housing?

In its scheme for Tyneside the English Commission used its power to relate areas and functions in the special review areas, whereas in West Yorkshire and the West Midlands it adhered to existing types of authorities. The Tyneside plan was for a new county authority which would embrace all of the Tyneside conurbation. Within the county would have been four county districts based on four county boroughs, Newcastle-on-Tyne, Tynemouth, South Shields and Gateshead, to be combined with adjacent lesser authorities for this purpose. The demotion of four county boroughs would be a most serious step, especially in the case of Newcastle which has a population of 270,000, but the Commission argued that only by the creation of a single authority covering the whole of Tyneside could the major planning problems of the area be solved, notably housing, the location of industry and the development of communications. The county authority would also be responsible for police, fire, ambulance and civil defence, but more personal services including education, health and welfare would remain with the four county districts which would have a wider range of functions than other second-tier authorities. Thus in Tyneside the Commission was suggesting not merely geographical changes but also a new division of responsibility between upper and lower tier authorities. However, the Minister (at this stage, Mr Crossman) rejected the Boundary Commission's advice because he preferred the idea of an all-purpose borough for the whole area. The matter was subsequently shelved pending the report of the Royal Commission.

A number of factors led to the decline of the English Commission. Wales is considered separately below. The morass of procedure for dealing with objectors strangled any impetus in its work. Some of its schemes seemed to be designed to arouse a maximum of ill-feeling while achieving a minimum of benefit. Was it wise to propose chopping Rutland into bits, rather than a simple amalgamation with Leicestershire? Does it really matter whether Lyme Regis is in Dorset or Devon? The Commission would have proceeded more speedily and probably with more influence had it concentrated always on major issues. But on major issues the Commission got little support from the Government. The reprieve of Rutland was the most glaring example. With only 25,000 people Rutland is forced to rely heavily on its neighbours to assist in the provision of secondary and further education, health and welfare services, police, fire and library facilities. Rutland is not so much a local authority as a purchaser of local government services. If Rutland continues what justification could there be for amalgamating other counties? Since each county borough has more inhabitants than Rutland, why should any county borough be demoted? Certainly, population is not the sole yardstick by which to measure whether an authority can provide efficient services, but population statistics do provide a simple, uncomplicated test which is persuasive to the public mind. After Rutland the Commission lost credibility and its status was further damaged when the Government refused its request to expand the Manchester and Merseyside Special Review Areas and so close the gap between them. This decision led to the resignation of one member of the Commission, Professor Ely Devons.

The final death blow to the Commission, and perhaps it was a happy release, came from the appearance of a Minister of Housing and Local Government who was determined to accomplish the radical reforms he thought necessary. Yet the Minister, Mr Crossman, still proceeded cautiously. He had been in office nearly a year before he made a major speech on the topic of structural reform. A few sentences of his address to the 1965 Conference of the Association of Municipal Corporations at Torquay are worth quoting. He argued that '. . . the whole structure of local government is out of date, that our county borough and county councils as at present organized are archaic institutions whose size and structure make them increasingly ill-adapted to fulfilling the immensely important functions with which they are charged. The greatest obstacle, in fact, which prevents efficient councils from retaining public confidence is the obsolete constitutional framework within which they had to operate.' From a responsible Minister these were striking words. One would expect them to herald immediate action. But the Minister was still hesitating. He confessed that his first intention on taking office was to wind up the English Boundary Commission and start again. Instead he announced that it would be necessary to appoint a 'powerful and impartial' committee to work out a policy on which the Commission's actions should be based.

The Boundary Commission's position by now was untenable. How could it continue to survey the country in detail, area by area, when the Minister proposed to establish a committee which would try to evolve principles to govern the Commission's actions? Ultimately, the Minister recognized the total impossibility of the situation. The English Commission was brought to an end in 1966 and was replaced by a new Royal Commission on Local Government which could start with a clean sheet while still making use of the vast stock of information which the Boundary Commission had collected.

Relatively few major reforms came from the Boundary Commission's seven years of endeavour. Its unfinished enquiries were abandoned and the Minister took no further action on most of the schemes already submitted to him. Likewise the county reviews were stopped in 1966 and changes only became effective in a few counties, e.g. Shropshire, which had proceeded most rapidly with this work.

In view of the widespread acceptance of the need to modernize structure and the substantial efforts spreading over twenty years to promote change, the lack of achievement requires explanation. Proponents of local government reform are automatic targets for certain lines of attack. They are said to be tidy-minded and over-willing to sacrifice established institutions and loyalties for the sake of dull uniformity. Certainly, reformers commonly fail to appreciate the extent and the value of local patriotism. Councillors who have given much service to a local authority cannot be expected to welcome its projected demise and they resent any implication that their council has been unable to carry out its duties with full efficiency. Local government officers, especially chief officials, fear for the effect of change on their personal status. It is commonly argued without any evidence that proposed alterations will have an adverse effect on the level of the rate poundage. Behind these forces of local opinion stand the national pressure groups, the associations of local authorities, ready to do what they can to safeguard the interests of their members. This is not to berate the associations: they were formed to protect the interests of their members, a task which they have carried through effectively. The difficulty is not merely that the associations object to change that adversely affects their own members but also that the counties and the boroughs have had diametrically opposed ideas as to the optimum pattern for local government. The Government has been weak in that it has been unwilling to enforce basic alterations in structure unless it can achieve a broad measure of agreement from the interests concerned. Politically the reform of local government is an awkward topic. Councillors and aldermen are leading figures in constituency parties and well able to make their views known to their local Member of Parliament. Faced with a strong backing of opinion which objects strenuously to some change proposed by a boundary commission, the local M.P. may well consider it prudent to support these protests. Indeed, on this matter it is difficult to apply the standard processes of party discipline which normally ensure that Government policy is accepted by the Commons – a difficulty which will recur when the report of the new Royal Commission is ripe for decision.

## THE ROYAL COMMISSION ON LOCAL GOVERNMENT

The Royal Commission was appointed in February, 1966, under the chairmanship of Lord Redcliffe-Maud with these terms of reference:

'To consider the structure of local government in England, outside Greater London, in relation to its existing functions; and to make recommendations for authorities and boundaries, and for functions and their division, having regard to the size and the character of areas in which these can be most effectively exercised and the need to sustain a viable system of democracy.'

It will be noted that this phraseology contains a hint of the perennial conflict between efficiency and democracy. The choice of chairman was also significant: one expects Lord Redcliffe-Maud to produce a structure which will be in harmony with the ideas of the earlier Maud Committee on the internal management of local authorities. The management board plan implies large units and the evidence presented to the Royal Commission has shown a concensus of opinion in favour of bigness.

The views of government departments presented to the Commission showed quite remarkable similarity. All favour larger units of local government in the interests of efficiency and uniformity. No doubt they feel that fewer local authorities would be easier to supervise. The Ministry of Transport wished for 30 to 40 major transport authorities to replace the present 823 highway authorities and 1,190 parking authorities. Indeed, all the departments favour 30 to 40 major authorities. How did these magic figures occur separately to so many minds? Within the overall figure of 30 to 40 authorities there was some variation of approach. Education sought a minimum population of at least 300,000 but Health was prepared to go down to 200,000. There was also difference about the need for second-tier authorities: Housing and Local Government accepted the need for a second-tier, the Treasury assumed all-purpose authorities while Transport was unsure – 'there is no advantage in creating lower-tier authorities in areas which could be adequately governed at first-tier level.'

As the government departments were so heavily in favour of larger units it is perhaps surprising that they wanted 30 to 40 major local authorities. Why not even fewer? It is clear that there is an earnest desire to avoid anything in the form of local government run by elected representatives at regional level, for this might impinge on the regional activities of departments and Regional Planning Boards and Councils. Elected regional bodies might wish to claim back some services now run by departments, e.g. hospitals, and they could also damage the status of the regional boards. The Department of Economic Affairs was particularly sensitive on this point: it argued that elected authorities could not take over the responsibilities of regional boards since, 'We cannot envisage a situation where central government is advised by local government'. To this the obvious rejoinder is 'Why?' Admittedly, an elected body would press strongly to attract maximum economic benefits for its region. So, presumably, does a nominated advisory board. The difference is that a nominated body operating in private should be more objective in its evaluation of problems and will cause less fuss if its advice is rejected.

Evidence from the associations of local authorities was less uniform but more forward looking than on previous occasions: delegation of county functions to second-tier authorities now attracts little interest. The County Councils Association naturally proposed a two-tier system in which the top-tier authorities should have a minimum of half a million population with second-tier authorities of 40,000 to 150,000 – the lower figure being appropriate for sparsely peopled areas. Had the C.C.A. suggested a lower figure for major authorities, they would have opened the way for an increasing number of large towns to claim independence and maintain existing county borough status. The suggested distribution of functions between upper and lower tiers was not greatly different from the present arrangements, except that no recommendation was made about the allocation of responsibility for personal health, children and welfare services. The Association of Municipal Corporations were much less specific. It urged a two-tier system of elected provincial and local authorities but did not specify population limits for each type of authority: the intention seemed to be that provinces should be smaller than the existing economic regions but larger than the top-tier bodies envisaged by government departments and the County Councils Association. The difference is explained by the fact that the A.M.C. proposed only a limited range of functions for their provinces. It would include planning and some further education, perhaps police, fire and water supply.

Each of the other local authority associations presented their views to the Royal Commission, so did many other organizations connected with local government as well as individual persons and local authorities. To summarize all this material would take a whole book. Much of it is special pleading for a particular interest but the whole body of evidence does provide an invaluable record of the activities of local authorities and thought about the future of local government.

A supplementary memorandum put in by the A.M.C. is worthy of special mention. It criticized the assumption that larger education authorities were necessarily more efficient or more generous in their standards of provision. It argued that the Department of Education and Science had taken as an article of faith that bigger means better without any supporting evidence. The A.M.C. produced detailed statistics to show that no such relationship existed, that the amount spent *per capita* on furniture, non-teaching staff, school health and inspection had no clear correlation to the size of authorities. In the smaller county boroughs the cost of provision of school meals was *lower* than in the largest county boroughs. A survey of the administrative experience of chief education officers showed that those in smaller authorities tended to have the greatest diversity of experience (though diversity of experience does not necessarily imply higher quality). And it argued convincingly that many valuable educational experiments had been initiated by the smaller education authorities, e.g. I.T.A. teaching methods in Oldham and the school dental service in Cambridge.

The view that education authorities require a minimum population of 300,000 implies that the London Boroughs are too small to be effective education authorities. Since these authorities were created as recently as 1963, and since minimum sizes of authority are generally thought of as being *higher* in densely populated areas, the 300,000 standard is open to a great deal of objection. Another problem concerning education that faces the Commission is whether education functions can be split between two tiers of authority. If an upper-tier authority is requisite for further education, must primary education also be provided by the same category of authority? The Departmental view has been that education is an inter-related whole and cannot be divided. The contrary view is that there is a clear break between school education and further education, both in relation to geographical location and the type and method of education provided. The question of whether a function can be divided also arises elsewhere – can house construction usefully be separated from house maintenance, can highway construction be divorced from traffic control? But it is in education that the divisibility of the service is a most crucial issue.

The dominant problem before the Commission is undoubtedly the size and nature of the top-tier units. A widely canvassed solution is the idea of the City Region, a concept ably advocated by Mr Derek Senior who was subsequently appointed a member of the Commission. The City Region plan aims to end the artificial divorce between town and countryside. Rural areas now require the same range and standard of service as urban areas and people living in the countryside regularly go to the principal town in their area for shopping, professional services, business purposes, cultural and leisure activities. It is argued, therefore, that local administrative areas should reflect this pattern of social living by dividing the country into some thirty areas based on the largest towns which would become major local government centres both for themselves and their surrounding hinterlands. It is clear that outside the main conurbations the towns do have fairly recognizable catchment areas often defined by the pattern of bus services: the small market towns provide a centre for weekly shopping and the larger towns are visited for other more specialized purposes. The City Region idea is attractive since it relates local government with social reality but, inevitably, there are difficulties in its practical application. It fits more easily in some parts of the country than in others. Brighton, Leicester, Norwich, Newcastle are natural centres for city region units, but how can the scheme be applied to Kent and Essex? The City Region plan also implies that existing county boundaries be disregarded. Does this matter? Perhaps county boundaries should be treated as mediaeval relics and deserve to be ignored. They do, however, affect the pattern of organization of many voluntary bodies. Examples of this can be seen from the London reorganization of 1963, where the Middlesex Cricket Club continues to exist despite the disappearance of Middlesex as an administrative unit. In a sense the Middlesex example underrates the problem because the area had long been swamped by metropolitan suburbia and loyalty to the county was negligible. But to tamper with other county boundaries would raise strong emotions. If Middlesex meant little to its inhabitants, Cornwall, for example, means a great deal. To state this problem is not to argue that county boundaries must be sacrosanct, but merely to recognize that the nomination of some towns, e.g. Plymouth, as the centre of a city region based on a realistic catchment area does provide special difficulties.

The main criticism of the City Region idea is quite different. Does it provide an area large enough for many important local government functions? In future, planning must be done on a wide scale; in particular land use, economic development, new towns and transportation all need to be looked at in regional terms. If the new local government units are inadequate for these tasks, then responsibility will be moved away from local government either to the central government or to new *ad hoc* agencies. The big region solution thus has great advantages over the city regions. It should also be simpler to arrange in terms of boundaries. New regional areas would be based more on an amalgamation of existing units and it would be easier to retain many traditional divisions. With, say, twelve big regional authorities, it is inevitable that the second-tier authorities would have an important part in the total system: whether second-tier units could have any significant tasks in the City Region scheme is far less clear. Are we facing the paradox that the way to keep local government as local as possible is to have bigger – much bigger – top-tier units?

In spite of this prospect there is little influential support, apart perhaps from the A.M.C., for still bigger units of local government. As noted above, the Civil Service seems to view anything approaching elected regional authorities as dangerous competitors, while local authorities as a whole have traditionally been averse to regionalism because it threatened their existing status. An institution yet unborn – and faced by strong established competitors – is necessarily short of powerful advocates. Certainly, the Bow Group and the Young Conservatives have issued pamphlets supporting elected regional bodies, but the balance of pressure appears to be against them. Even the A.M.C. advocacy of provincial authorities is half-hearted; it springs not from enthusiasm for the idea but from an unhappy acceptance of the fact that all existing county boroughs cannot retain complete independence so, to prevent amalgamation with counties, the A.M.C. seeks to put above them authorities with a limited range of functions.

Any discussion of the reshaping of local government structure must concentrate on the nature of future top-tier authorities. Yet the other end of the scale, the small community, should not be wholly forgotten. Is there to be any place at all for a third-tier council? Or should the parish disappear completely as a local government unit? In many rural areas the parish council is still a stimulus to interest in public affairs and a useful channel of opinion. There is no reason why this representative function should be taken away, especially as its value in sounding out opinion will increase if second-tier authorities are made much larger. Whether a parish should have any executive tasks is another question. One possibility is that a parish council should have no duties imposed on it but should be permitted to levy a rate on the parish to provide amenities, e.g. playing fields, bus shelters, etc., should it wish to do so. These matters may seem petty in comparison with the wider issues discussed above. But there is a sense of social cohesion in village communities which helps to compensate for the lack of facilities and opportunities of town life. Parish councils reinforce this cohesion, so there is a case for their retention.

## WALES

Public opinion has also inhibited change in Wales. The problem here is that the counties, especially those in central Wales, have small populations which are scattered across a beautiful, but often infertile, countryside; in consequence, rateable values are low and the local authorities have inadequate financial resources to maintain a standard of public services comparable with that enjoyed in other areas. The 1958 Commission for Wales intended to deal with this situation by a drastic plan of county amalgamations which would have reduced the number of Welsh counties from thirteen to seven. Anglesey alone was to remain intact. Inevitably, the plan was hotly opposed in Wales. Local patriotism was incensed by the complete disregard of existing county boundaries and some of the new counties proposed were both large and inconvenient in shape. The Welsh Commission itself regarded the proposals as less than the optimum for it argued in its Report, 'that an investigation of local government which is to be fully effective must go beyond a consideration of its boundaries to that of its structure, its functions and its finance.' This need is commonly stressed by students of local government and it was, of course, central to the ideas of the ill-fated Boundary Commission of 1945. It is also a principle that Ministers in the past have been reluctant to accept. However, in 1964, the Minister of Housing and Local Government announced that a fresh examination of Welsh local government would have to be made embracing both finance and functions. Meanwhile, the scheme for seven counties was rejected, so the Welsh Commission's work proved fruitless save for minor adjustments to county borough boundaries. Subsequently an inter-departmental Working Party was established to review Welsh problems and it undertook a wide range of informal consultations. Its conclusions were published in 1967. The main proposals were that Merthyr Tydfil should cease to be a county borough and that the counties be reduced from thirteen to five. However, the plan was to amalgamate counties rather than divide them as proposed by the previous Commission. The three new counties suggested are:

Gwynedd – an amalgamation of Denbighshire, Flintshire, Anglesey, Caernarvonshire and Merionethshire.

Powys – an amalgamation of Montgomeryshire, Radnorshire and Breconshire.

Dyfed – an amalgamation of Cardiganshire, Carmarthenshire and Pembrokeshire.

Glamorgan and Monmouthshire, renamed Gwent, were to remain the same except that the Rhymney Valley be transferred to Monmouth. Thus with the three remaining county boroughs, Cardiff, Newport and Swansea, there would be eight major local authorities in Wales, with Newport and Powys being significantly weaker than the others. At the second-tier level the report would reduce the number of councils from the present 164 to 36. Third-tier parishes would be reorganized by the new counties and might be called common councils (an unfortunate derogatory term?), they could also be established in urban areas if the inhabitants so wished. In the sphere of finance the main reform suggested is that counties become rating authorities with districts precepting on counties. Further consideration would have to be given to the extent of delegation of county powers to districts.

If action is taken on the Welsh proposals prior to parallel decisions for England, the future pattern of local government in Wales may diverge from that of England. This could well be appropriate since the problems of Wales are in some degree different.

## LONDON

The task of reforming local government in the London area was unique in magnitude. Over eight million people, roughly a sixth of the population of England and Wales, are clustered together in the Greater London conurbation. In 1957 the Government decided that the problem was so vast as to need separate treatment; a Royal Commission was appointed to study the complexities of the metro-politan area which was therefore excluded from the purview of the Local Government Commission for England. The central difficulty was the absence of any local authority which embraced the whole of the Greater London area. The London County Council inherited its boundary from the Metropolitan Board of Works which was established in 1855; while it represents the geographical realities of a century ago, this boundary has no relevance to the facts of the present day. London spilled over into large sections of Kent, Surrey, Hertford, Essex and the whole of Middlesex. Little more than a third of the population of Greater London lived within the L.C.C. area, and the L.C.C. population of 3,200,000 was still declining slowly. There were also three county boroughs in Greater London, Croydon, East Ham and West Ham, so it followed that nine top-tier authorities in the London area were each responsible for broad issues of plan-ning policy. No single local authority could have a synoptic view of the issues connected with the redevelopment and zoning of Greater London, the movement of population and the construction of main traffic arteries. In the counties surrounding the L.C.C. there were no fewer than fourteen county districts with more than 100,000 inhabi-tants. These authorities, had they been situated elsewhere, would have had an automatic claim to county borough status. As it was, the larger county districts in suburban London commonly shared in county functions through a system of delegation by the county councils. Delegation is a somewhat cumbrous arrangement which runs smoothly only if there is full co-operation between the parties thereto. In many cases it has worked well: elsewhere, notably in Middlesex, it did not. Inside the L.C.C. area were the City of Lon-don and the twenty-eight Metropolitan Boroughs created in 1899, which were also of uneven size – Wandsworth had 338,000 inhabi-tants and Holborn had 21,000. L.C.C. delegation to the Metropolitan Boroughs was negligible.

This in brief outline was the situation facing the Royal Commission. Its Report, Cmnd. 1164 of 1960, unanimously urged drastic changes. The Commission was of opinion that a Council for Greater London should be established to be responsible for overall planning, main roads, fire and ambulance services. It would also share responsibility for education, housing, planning applications and certain other services with a new type of second-tier authority – Greater London Boroughs. These Greater London Boroughs would have the status and constitution of municipal boroughs except that the City of London would be permitted to retain its present institutions. The Commission's scheme envisaged fifty-two of these Boroughs with populations between 100,000 and 250,000 – except, again, for the City of London: they would be responsible for health and welfare services, child care, local roads and libraries, in addition to the duties shared with the Council for Greater London. Reorganization on this scale involved the disappearance of the L.C.C., Middlesex and three county boroughs, substantial loss of territory and rateable value by four county councils, and extensive amalgamations of county districts and Metropolitan Boroughs. It is thus not surprising that this Report also aroused substantial opposition.

In this instance, however, the Government were not deflected by local hostility. They accepted the broad lines of the Royal Commission's Report and the London Government Act, 1963, now provides an opportunity for the co-ordinated planning of the whole metropolitan area. There were some modifications to the Commission's proposals. The number of London Boroughs was reduced from 52 to 32. There were two reasons for this change: first, some fringe areas were excluded from the London area altogether and remain in Surrey and Essex, and second, and far more important, the minimum population of London Boroughs was doubled. This rise to 200,000 was due partly to the further decision that London Boroughs shall have full powers over education – save in the former L.C.C. territory where a committee of the Greater London Council, representing the area concerned, has this responsibility.

The challenge facing the new Greater London Council is formidable and exciting. Its size and scope dwarf all other of our local authorities. There is now the chance to provide cohesive direction to the development of the national capital and its environs. Further, London government is a potential model for local government reform elsewhere in England, which could lead to the adoption of large regions with second-tier authorities exercising wide powers.

*Chapter IX*

---

# LOCAL GOVERNMENT AND SOCIETY

### THE PATTERN OF PRESSSURES

It is important to visualize local government in the context of the sum total of its social relationships. This can be assisted by means of a diagram. The chart on the next page is a sort of map which shows how a local authority fits in with the public, with central government, with political parties and other voluntary organizations. It shows the flow of pressure and experience between these parts of the social system – the channels through which demands are made upon a local council, how the council itself may try to exert influence, how the council's services may arouse public reaction and how central government agencies help to supervise local services. Inevitably the diagram involves much simplification. It omits some links which are not immediately significant for the individual local authority. A chart cannot demonstrate the indirect way in which voters can affect the election of aldermen. Nor is it possible to convey the complex relationship within the council organization between elected members and officers. But it does show the essential circularity of local administration – how people make demands on local authorities and subsequently react to how their demands are met. The chart is also able to distinguish those formal relationships which are enshrined in law. Statutory relationships are indicated by a continuous line and informal ones by a broken line. Most of these links operate on a two way basis, e.g. the local authority associations have an effect on government policy but the government also has an impact on the attitudes of the associations. It may sometimes be a matter of doubt which is having the greater influence on the other. Thus while local opinion may conceivably take note of the speeches of councillors acting as local opinion leaders, the constitutional position is that the voters choose councillors to represent local opinion.

It should be remembered that the diagram is purely *descriptive*. It does nothing to explain what sort of decision a council will make in any given set of circumstances. This is because it is not possible to quantify pressures or to assess precisely the effect of influences pulling in opposite directions. The diagram is merely an aid to understanding the social situation within which local government must work. In partcular it illustrates how various voluntary organizations can have an impact on local administration. The churches

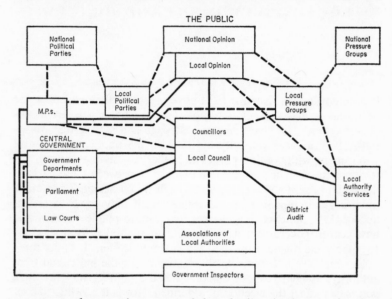

are among the most important of these bodies; in the past they had a dominating position in relation to education. The Lord's Day Observance Society may be stung into action if a local authority arranges or permits some activity on a Sunday. Tenants associations are today among the most vigorous local groups and may organize protests if council house rents are increased. And there are a mass of other bodies urging a wide variety of policies on local authorities – progress in education, anti-fluoridation, rural preservation and so on. The interest of voluntary organizations in local government appears to be growing. They are a peculiarly valuable element in maintaining a spirit of local democracy as they frequently promote causes that cut across the lines of political party policies.

At least two other aspects of the chart demand comment. It shows that the local council decides policy in relation to local services, but it must not be forgotten that the experience of being a member of a local authority and gaining knowledge about local government functions may itself influence members of local councils. A new councillor may think that better standards of service should be provided; after some months on the council he may change his view as he comes to appreciate the financial and other difficulties. Alternatively, a new councillor may be critical of policies he feels to be extravagant; on a fuller acquaintanceship with the benefits derived from these policies he may come to accept that they are justified. The chart also implies that local experience of local services has an influence on behaviour at elections; if voters are satisfied with the services they will be content to keep the same councillors – otherwise they will seek to make changes. This is the way in which local democracy is supposed to work. In earlier years the theory may have had some connection with practice. Now wherever politics dominates local elections, voters react on party lines according to their views on the performance of the national government. So there may be a big change in the membership and political balance of a local authority, not because of dissatisfaction with its policies or the quality of its administration, but because of reactions to Government activity.

## CENTRAL-LOCAL RELATIONS

The development of political controversy in relation to local affairs has also tended to link central and local government more closely together. This is not simply a matter of national parties contesting local elections or of the control of a council's policy by the 'caucus' of the local majority party. It is also the case that Ministers often claim political credit for the activities of local authorities, especially in connection with building houses and schools, in spite of the fact that a large part of this construction has been carried out by councils dominated by their political opponents. Ministers also press the development of certain policies that affect the way local authorities carry out their responsibilities, e.g. green belt preservation, old people's housing, the sale of council houses and, not least, comprehensive secondary education.

It is often argued that such ministerial influence is undemocratic in that the wishes of locally elected representatives can be overridden by the edict of a remote organization in Whitehall. Yet this argument is not easy to sustain. If democracy is defined as the acceptance of majority opinion, it would seem to be as democratic to follow the will of the Minister who represents the national majority as it is to follow the wishes of those who represent but a local majority. If democracy is defined in terms of paying attention to local opinion, then the smaller the unit of opinion the more attention should be paid to its desires. Should a parish council be allowed to override a county council? Should the representatives of a ward be entitled to insist that a different policy be applied to their ward as opposed to the other wards in the borough? Financial considerations apart, claims of this sort are a prescription for anarchy. Here is a dilemma. A healthy democracy needs strong, vigorous and independent-minded local government genuinely able to exercise initiative and judgement. At the same time local authorities get massive monetary aid from the Treasury and are expected to assist in promoting national social purposes.

The independence of local authorities has been deeply undermined by their reliance on financial help from the central government. There is no doubt that local rates are a most unsatisfactory form of taxation for there is no certain correlation, as there is with income tax, between the amount an individual has to pay and his capacity to pay. Resistance to paying higher rates, aggravated by the unfairness of the system, has effectively reduced the taxing capacity of local councils, and has led to incessant demands for more state subsidies. It is widely argued that education – easily the most expensive local government service – is a national service and, as such, should be financed entirely by the national Exchequer. Yet how far would it continue to be a local government service if education authorities had no financial responsibility save to the Secretary of State for Education? Meanwhile, local control of administration and expenditure, albeit constrained by Whitehall, does preserve an element of community responsibility, pride and satisfaction. Services provided by the central government do not inspire similar attitudes. The health service is a natural example. There is general dissatisfaction with the hospital service – not necessarily with the individual contributions of doctors, nurses and hospital administrators – but with the scale of provision as a whole. There is a feeling that 'they', the anonymous, abstract and unknown controllers of the system, ought to effect various improvements. Controllers of the local health and welfare services are not unknown; if there are serious complaints, they will soon hear of them. Where cost is the obstacle to meeting the complaint, the difficulty is more readily appreciated. 'To improve the health centre means putting the rate up,' is a statement which carries a more meaningful choice than 'To improve hospitals means an increase in taxation.' It is not merely that the national purse may appear bottomless, it is also the case that any successful local claim on national resources has a net benefit to the local community. So long as cost is linked to a local tax, the cost-benefit relationship is realistic. Whenever the Government takes over a local service it puts a premium on grumbling by destroying local financial responsibility.

Lack of rate revenue alone has so far not deprived local authorities of any functions. Nor is it any longer the sole economic cause of greater central supervision. As a major public consumer of labour and capital resources, local government is required to keep in step with the changing face of the Government's economic policy. Wages and salary levels of local authorities will be influenced by the national incomes policy; the nature and extent of capital expenditure on local schools, housing, roads, swimming baths, etc. will have to fit broadly into a national scheme of priorities. All public bodies are expected to co-operate in freezes and squeezes or any other general measures that Ministers feel necessary to promote the national economic interest. The nineteenth-century desire to achieve minimum standards throughout the country in relation to basic services such as poor relief and elementary education has tended to develop also into the imposition of maximum standards and, indeed, to an overall pattern of uniformity. As local authorities receive so much national financial aid this equality of provision is easily justified on grounds of fair distribution of the national taxpayer's money. Uniformity also requires that because smaller and weaker authorities need some degree of technical guidance the same must be applied to larger authorities with well qualified staff for whom such aid is unnecessary.

In essence, the status of local government has been eroded in this century by the development of a highly centralized system of public administration. This is the product of interlocking factors: a country that is densely populated but relatively small in area; the cultural, financial and political supremacy of London; the firmly entrenched two-party system that gives the Cabinet a secure parliamentary majority; the acceptance by both parties of welfare policies which they are determined to control nationally.

The Maud Committee accepted this centralized pattern and proposed to strengthen it still further. The Government was recommended to see if it were possible to nominate a single Minister to be responsible for co-ordinating its policy in relation to local authorities. On the other side, the Committee wanted the establishment of a Local Government Central Office to promote research, operate a central staffing organization and conduct negotiations with the central government. Such an office would take over a large part of the present functions of the local authority associations. These proposals are a logical step ahead in the further unification of public administration. Yet there is a danger to the creation of a main official channel of communication. It may well be more efficient; it may also become rather remote from the individual local authority. And any agreement reached in this central channel would be difficult to over-turn in Parliament or anywhere else.

There is a case for urging that these centripetal forces should be resisted. Strong reasons can be advanced against national interven-tion in local affairs, notably on matters of detail. Every increase in central control requires more staff in national offices to check what local authorities are doing. Not merely does this cost money, but it adds to delay. Each new item in the catalogue of supervision means a further loss of local responsibility. Both councillors and local gov-ernment officers can plead with some justification that it is not their fault if something goes amiss since they are acting under central direction. Distant control must be frustrating. It can develop a feel-ing among vigorous and able people that service in local government as elected representatives or salaried officers is not worthwhile. The claim for clear – if limited – independence for local government was stated by the Local Government Manpower Committee in 1950, '. . . local authorities are responsible bodies competent to discharge their own functions and though they may be statutory bodies through which Government policy is given effect and operate to a large extent with Government money, they exercise their responsibilities in their own right, not ordinarily as agents for Government Depart-ments. It follows that the objective should be to leave as much as possible . . . to the local authority and to concentrate the Depart-ment's control at key points where it can most effectively discharge its responsibilities for Government policy and financial administra-tion.' This type of sentiment attracts some support from politicians, especially when in opposition. In terms of actual legislation, one is left with the impression that the recommendation of the Manpower Committee has been ignored. To take just one example: Section 8 of the Public Libraries and Museums Act, 1964, permits the Secretary of State for Education and Science to decide the scale of fines for books overdue from a public library. It is impossible to provide adequate justification for a control of such a petty nature.

The latest proposals to streamline planning administration, how-ever, amount to a distinct check to the centralizing tendency. There is to be less detailed Ministry supervision over local development plans and the inspectors who hold planning appeals will be em-powered to take decisions themselves instead of merely preparing recommendations for Ministerial consideration. At the same time more emphasis is being placed on the need for local planners to consult local opinion. Why are these changes being made? Is it that national administration now has greater faith in the wisdom of local authorities? The more realistic explanation is that the highly centralized system of approvals and appeal decisions has been breaking down through the sheer volume of work. Delays in obtaining Ministry decisions lengthened so greatly that some simplification of the pattern of administration became inevitable.

## *VIRES* AND DISTRICT AUDIT

The basic legal constraint on local authorities is the doctrine of *ultra vires* which requires them to be able to provide specific legal authorization for all their actions. The principle was not imposed on local government by a deliberate act of national policy; it evolved from judicial decisions which limited the activities of railway companies to business directly connected with the running of a railway. The argument was that railways were authorized by Acts of Parliament and, as statutory corporations, they must be restricted to the purposes for which they were created. Local authorities were immediately involved because they are all statutory corporations, apart from boroughs outside London. Whether boroughs are also governed by the *ultra vires* rule has been discussed above but the essential fact is that boroughs behave as if they are so restricted. Thus local authorities are fettered by a legal rule that has not received specific authorization from Parliament: it is, moreover, a rule that the Courts have interpreted very strictly.

There can, of course, be two views on the desirability of the *ultra vires* principle. Certainly, it inhibits enterprise and experiment; it also removes opportunities for extravagance and folly. Were councils freed from this restraint they would still be subject to the ballot-box and if electors were not satisfied by the reasons offered for inflated rate-demands a change of councillors and council policy would become highly likely. A few adventures or misadventures by local authorities could rapidly reduce public apathy about their activities. One has the feeling, however, that the *ultra vires* principle is now widely accepted by Ministers, Parliament, local officials and councillors with a certain sense of relief in that it prevents unorthodoxy and fresh difficulties. Optional activities are normally those which cause the greatest friction, partly because they provide obvious targets in any economy drive and partly because their continuation depends wholly on the will of the local council, and there is no possibility of pushing off responsibility on the central government. Some local disputes about cultural expenditure have attracted widespread publicity, e.g. the Bournemouth Symphony Orchestra, the Nottingham Playhouse and the Edinburgh Festival: in the case of Edinburgh the trouble has not been solely financial but has also been caused by the nature of some of the 'fringe' events associated with the Festival. In the nineteen-twenties Labour Members of Parliament supported a Local Authorities (Enabling) Bill which sought to give larger local authorities discretionary powers to promote trading and cultural activities. Yet in office successive Labour Governments have shown no enthusiasm whatever for this sort of legislation. The issue seemed to be dead. However, the Local Government (Financial Provisions) Act, 1963, allows a local authority to incur expenditure up to the amount of a penny rate for any purpose which in its opinion would benefit the area, provided that such activity is not subject to other statutory provisions. Thus the District Auditor will not be able to make surcharges for trifling amounts. So far there is little evidence that the new power has been used to a significant extent but the margin of freedom allowed by the penny rate limit is too narrow to permit startling developments.

The Maud Committee suggested that a further relaxation be allowed so that local authorities be given a 'general competence' to do whatever they feel to be in the interests of their areas, subject to not encroaching on the spheres of other public bodies and to 'appropriate safeguards for the protection of public and private interests'. The proposal appears radical but it is also extremely vague. The idea of safeguarding private interests could inhibit any scheme to undertake commercial activities, even cultural and recreational provision could conflict with existing business interests. There would also be widespread objection to granting any right to subsidize local political or religious organizations. However, some foreign countries do have 'general competence' clauses. The idea has obvious attractions and could do much to enliven local government. But there are great difficulties in the way of giving this plan a precise legal form.

Were local authorities to receive wider powers of this nature the existing character of district audit would necessarily be changed. The Maud Committee recognized this consequence and urged that the District Auditor be deprived of the right to impose surcharges. This suggestion is popular in local government circles as councillors and officials do not like the threat of surcharge for obvious reasons. Councillors also resent the concept of surcharge since it enables a government official – albeit one independent of Ministers and exercising a quasi-judicial function – to impose penalties on elected representatives for using their judgment in the way they think best. It must be remembered that the Auditor is not concerned only with accuracy and probity. Surcharges can fall on improper and *ultra vires* expenditure and also on expenditure that is held by the Auditor to be unreasonable. This situation derives from a general rule of law that requires public bodies to exercise discretion given to them by statute 'reasonably', so that unreasonable expenditure becomes illegal expenditure. In the past elected councillors have contested the claim that the Auditor be enabled to override their judgments on the nature of what is reasonable in this context. Councillors are answerable to electors: the District Auditor is responsible to no one as the Minister of Housing and Local Government will not accept responsibility for his decisions which cannot, therefore, be effectively challenged in Parliament.

Appeal against a surcharge can be made to the High Court or, if the sum involved is less than £500, there is an option of appealing to the Court or the Minister. There is another check on the Auditor in that the Minister can give specific sanction to items of local authority expenditure which has the effect of removing them from the jurisdiction of the Auditor. While these safeguards are valuable they are still poor comfort to councillors. They do not remove the basic complaint that a public official can over-rule the decisions of elected representatives. In the nineteen-twenties George Lansbury and the Labour group on the Poplar Borough Council were in conflict with the Auditor for years because the latter objected to Poplar paying wages above those obtainable elsewhere for comparable work. Surcharges levied on Lansbury and his colleagues year after year were unpaid: in consequence, the Audit (Local Authorities) Act, 1927, provided that any person surcharged more than £500 should be disqualified from membership of any local authority for five years.

Today the District Auditor seems much less of an ogre than he did forty years ago. On average, there are three cases a year of surcharge on councillors and the great majority of these relate to claims for loss of time and expenses. The Auditor rarely raises issues about the reasonableness of expenditure. Perhaps there is less need for him to do so. Local authorities are now conditioned to accept central directions through a wide range of administrative controls, and so are less likely to engage in unorthodox spending. Political conflicts over local government services are not so acute as in the nineteen-twenties – partly because public assistance has become a matter for national administration. Some people in a position to judge also believe that the Auditor is now more elastic in his approach to *ultra vires* issues. Also, instead of imposing a surcharge, he may give a private warning that certain expenditure is questionable and should not be repeated.

The Auditor can still serve a useful function even if he loses the power to surcharge. He already gives much advice to officers of local authorities on administrative methods, and can pass on the experience of one authority to another. He would still be required to report to authorities on any discrepancies found in the accounts. He could still criticize publicly the financial policy of a council. Such a report might provoke a ratepayer to initiate legal action against a council on the grounds that certain actions were *ultra vires*, although if general competence powers were granted the scope for such actions would be limited. But the Auditor would not, personally, hold councillors in thrall, and it would be for councillors to decide what action, if any, to take on his reports. There will be those who complain that to restrict the Auditor's duties in this way is to remove a potent check on the activities of local councils. It seems fair to reply that there is more danger of local government being checked by too many controls than there is of it running riot through lack of restraints.

### PEOPLE AND LOCAL GOVERNMENT

It is a commonplace that we live in mass society. All major units of social organization, with the family as the main exception, tend to increase in size. Employers are fewer in number and operate on a larger scale; trade unions are fewer and larger; towns, schools, hospitals, even universities, get bigger. Government departments grow larger and local authorities are set to follow the same trend, although up to now their progress in this direction has been halting. Taken together, all this must have a great psychological impact on the individual. There can be a tendency to feel lost in the crowd, to experience a sense of helplessness in face of major social pressures, to lose interest in community problems, indeed, perhaps to lose part of a sense of responsibility for one's own actions. In a word, a dangerous possibility can develop – some would say has developed – for the individual to become alienated from society as a whole. The public support given to youth organizations and other cultural, social and recreational activities is in some measure a recognition of this danger and an attempt to counteract it.

Local government, as the smallest and most approachable unit in our system of public administration, should be able to play a major role in breaking down the invisible barriers between the individual and society. It is easier to make an impact on local decisions than it is to affect national decisions. It is easier to make complaints about local administration in the sense that the persons responsible are more immediately accessible. National government has now felt obliged to appoint a Parliamentary Commissioner or Ombudsman to look into complaints about administration – not complaints about policy – forwarded to him by Members of Parliament on behalf of constituents. Again, this is a move to try and overcome an evil of mass society, that the shortcomings of bureaucracy may not always be able to be held in check by the traditional means of parliamentary question and debate. The question now arises whether local authorities, at least the large ones, should establish similar machinery. It can well be argued that many matters on which the sense of personal grievance may be greatest, concerning planning, housing, education, health and welfare provisions, come within the ambit of local government rather than national government. If national civil servants are liable to be investigated by an independent official acting in response to a complaint from an aggrieved person – why should not this practice be extended to local authorities? Not every local authority need have its own investigating commissioner; one commissioner could deal with a group of adjacent authorities.

This idea has some attractions. But local government already suffers so many checks and restraints that it must be a matter of opinion whether an extra one is desirable. The parallel with central government is also far from exact. Local authority administration is on a much smaller scale than national administration and the chance that serious mistakes will go uncorrected should be substantially less. At Westminster the Member of Parliament is physically remote from civil servants; he will not know them personally except by rarest chance; he will scarcely if ever meet them. Traditionally, Members have sent in complaints to Ministers who will have a political, if not a personal, motive for asserting that the administrative processes of their departments are tantamount to perfection. Virtually none of this applies to local government. Councillors know their chief officials and take complaints to them direct. They are, indeed, concerned with the details of administration through their committee work. Do local authorities need Ombudsmen since, in a sense, they have plenty already through the presence of elected representatives? But it is not wholly clear that a councillor can always fill the role of an Ombudsman; if he receives a complaint about a decision reached in one of his committees, he is being asked to investigate one of his own actions. Were committees to cease to deal with administrative detail and personal cases, as the Maud Committee wish, this difficulty would disappear. Indeed, the Maud Report hopes that if councillors are freed from spending so much time in committees, they would be freer to deal with complains and, like M.P.s, they would press complaints on members of the management board or on principal officers. The Maud concept does not require backbench councillors to be divorced from administration but to be connected with it through complaints rather than as decision-makers. One fears that it would not be easy for the older councillors to adjust their

attitudes to fit this new role. Nevertheless, a case can be made in
theory to show that this change in a councillor's function would
help him to act as a first link between an aggrieved individual and the
process of public administration. But Maud also favours limiting
the number of councillors. If we also have bigger and fewer councils,
the number of personal links between the man in the street and local
government could be cut severely.

It is vital for democracy that the claims and grievances of citizens
be dealt with equitably. This cannot mean that all grievances should
be satisfied and all claims accepted. It does require that complaints
be reviewed impartially and that where one claim is given preference
over another real justification can be found for the decision. Thus if
a council house is allocated to Brown rather than to Smith, it must
be because Brown has greater need of accommodation, because he
has been evicted or is living under more crowded conditions or some
similar reason – not because Brown has a friend or relative on the
council or because he has bribed an official. In Britain these principles are understood and accepted. There is a tendency to feel that
administrative abuses are so rare as not to constitute a problem.
While corruption and other patent abuse is infrequent, there are still
many cases of administrative error, failure of communication and
lack of understanding. Local government does show concern and
respect for individuals and is well placed to set an example for
central government in these matters because of the smaller, more
intimate scale of its operations. However, as the units of local administration get bigger, the sense of alienation of the individual from
local government must grow; the councillor, like the M.P., may become more divorced from administration. As this happens the case
for a local Ombudsman will demand more attention. Certainly there
will be increasing need for local public relations machinery and well
recognized channels for the receipt of complaints.

At present there is extreme public apathy about local government.
This is fully demonstrated by the research undertaken by the Government Social Survey for the Maud Committee. Over a quarter of
those interviewed by the Survey were unable to name *any* service
provided by their borough or district council: in county areas, the
position was worse as nearly half the interviewees apparently knew
nothing of the county's services. People in London Boroughs and
rural districts were the worst informed; in the metropolis men and
women are lost in the mass society and in the countryside the county
council is not so much impersonal as remote. Under one-fifth of
those interviewed by the Social Survey remembered having ap-
proached a councillor for advice. This picture of indifference is not

surprising. Life is short and the potential range of human endeavour and interest is vast. It is not unreasonable to feel that there are other and better things to do than to concern oneself with the problems of local government. Apathy can be a measure of contentment. If people are satisfied with social conditions why should they bother about them?

But apathy may be caused by alienation and ignorance rather than contentment. The nature of possible improvements may be unknown; when produced they may be warmly appreciated although not widely demanded in advance. If local government is to flourish it must take some trouble to educate those of the public willing to listen. Why not circulate to all households after each election the names and addresses of council members, together with a note of their committee assignments? Anyone who calls in at a council office in search of this information will not always find it is easy to obtain. Since the Public Bodies (Admission to Meetings) Act, 1960, the public have had a right to attend council meetings and meetings of education committees and divisional executives unless they are excluded by a specific resolution because publicity would be prejudicial to particular items of business. Equally the press and the broadcasting organizations have a right to be present. This, however, is not enough. The press should be admitted, whenever possible, to committee meetings and be provided with agendas in advance. Attempts should be made to explain the major decisions facing a council to the public at large, possibly by issuing local White Papers on the analogy of Government White Papers. Of course, where an issue becomes political it is often better party tactics to reach a decision quickly rather than stimulate public argument. Local and regional radio and television stations could do more to provoke interest in council activities. However, councillors and local government officers often treat the mass communications media with reserve because of a desire to avoid controversies.

The educational role of local government is a major support for our whole democratic system. When people come to understand the intricacies of local problems they are better equipped to understand the tasks of national government. The limited but still substantial number of men and women elected to take local government decisions have a fuller appreciation of the responsibilities of Ministers, M.P.s, judges and senior civil servants. Participation in the process of government at local level may stir unfortunate feelings of pride and prestige, but it also enhances knowledge and judgement and provides a channel of communication between government and governed without which no democracy can flourish.

Thus apathy produces twin dangers. If unchecked it may lead to deterioration of standards of services and permit the erosion of democratic safeguards. One old saying is always worth requoting: the secret of liberty is eternal vigilance. A test that should always be applied to any scheme to reform local government is whether it will increase or reduce public participation in its affairs. To give local authorities greater freedom of action in the form of general competence powers or to allow them wider discretion in other ways is to increase their impact on society and should arouse much interest. Alternatively, to have many fewer and much larger local authorities with a great reduction in the number of elected councillors will surround local government with greater anonymity: points of personal contact with individuals in mass society will be lessened. This is not to argue that the 'participation' test can be the sole or dominant criterion of policy, but it is an aspect of decision-making that may be given too little weight in face of considerations of administrative convenience.

## PAYMENT OF COUNCILLORS

To finish this book with a discussion on whether councillors should be paid may appear a little perverse. Is this not a question of secondary importance? Although the issue is rather narrower than many of the subjects examined above, the decision made on this topic will perhaps in a curious way do more than anything to influence the future tone of local government. It is certain to arouse much controversy partly because the issue is, or appears to be, very simple and partly because it will arouse suspicions about motivation – the sort of thing which enters into every-day discussion in the majority of homes.

The case for making payments is strong. Unless some financial recompense is available for councillors, many people who must spend the greater part of their time earning a living are perforce unable to offer their services. Apart from authorities small enough to be able to hold all meetings in the evenings, this limits the field of recruitment for councillors to housewives, retired people, the self-employed and those fortunate enough to have sympathetic employers willing to release them for local government work. The loss of time allowances introduced in 1948 have done little to help the situation; for able young executives and professional people the allowance is inadequate to compensate for the probable loss of earnings, especially as service on a local council may well damage prospects of promotion. Elected representatives naturally spend varying amounts of time on council work; their burden will depend on their personal inclinations, the size of the authority and their status within it. In the larger authorities, leading councillors and aldermen, including the chairmen of major committees, already devote a great deal of time each week to public service. For some these duties become virtually a full-time occupation. Why should we expect all this effort without significant financial cost to the community? If we want our councillors to fairly represent all sections of the community, particularly if we want younger and able councillors, it can be claimed that some kind of payment must be made.

The contrary case is also formidable. Payment would damage our valuable tradition of honorary public service. There is no wide demand that it should be introduced. Indeed, the Social Survey report to the Maud Committee showed that both councillors and ex-councillors are generally hostile to the idea: the Report also showed that lack of time rather than financial reasons was the main barrier to the recruitment of young, well-educated councillors. Payment would introduce a new and unpleasant question of motivation. All council candidates would be open to the sneer that they wished to be elected to get easy money. Were this type of attitude to become prevalent, it is probable that many people would be deterred from standing and some present councillors might drop out. Payment would increase the burden on the local rate and is thus unlikely to be popular with ratepayers. There are also difficult questions about how much should be paid and who should be paid. If the sums involved are substantial and designed to attract people of ability, the operation will be costly and there can be no guarantee that people of the requisite calibre will come forward – or that they will be elected. Large payments could well attract the wrong sort of person to council work. On the other hand, if the amounts offered are little more than a pittance, councils may still be dominated by retired persons or those with inadequate ability and experience. The dilemma here is inescapable. The question of who should be paid is also difficult. If all members are paid, again the cost will be high. And where elections are dominated by political parties, nomination by a party committee to a 'safe' seat would be tantamount to awarding the money. If only major chairmen and councillors are paid, then the councillors themselves award money to some of their colleagues. In either case, new categories of patronage are opened up. Nominations may then be made for the wrong reason: X may be chosen rather than Y on compassionate grounds – because it is known that he is in greater need of the money, perhaps because he has retired. There is one other disturbing prospect. A paid councillor may feel that he should intervene more often in matters of routine administration to prove to himself and others that he is earning his official salary.

In May, 1966, the Maud Committee issued an interim report concerned specifically with payments to elected members. The introduction of salaries was not recommended but the Committee reserved its position on payments to council and committee chairmen. Changes in the present system of allowances were proposed to make the scheme far more flexible. Members should not have to submit detailed claims; instead local authorities should be free to prescribe an annual flat expenses allowance of which the member could claim the whole or a part at his discretion. The allowance should cover loss of remunerative time, subsistence and travelling expenses, overheads such as postage, stationery, telephone and secretarial help and other incidental expenses incurred in performance of public duties. The loss of remuneration element was to be limited by a recognition that members may have to make some financial sacrifice through service on a council. Finally, the scale of this comprehensive allowance should be fixed not by the Government but by each local authority. No action so far has been taken on these proposals. It seems a pity that the Maud Committee separated the matter of payments from their other and wider considerations: obviously the interim report was produced in response to outside pressure. Their scheme for more generous expense allowances is a compromise. Under it some members would presumably get considerable payments, part of which would certainly be judged by the Inland Revenue as being liable to income tax.

The Committee in its final report said that part-time salaries should be made to members of the proposed management boards in addition to the expenses allowance for all councillors described above. The amount of this part-time salary would be fixed by the Minister of Housing and Local Government and be related to salaries paid to part-time members of public boards of a commercial character. In view of the measure of responsibility intended to be undertaken by management boards, this plan to pay their members seems inevitable. Yet it is still open to most of the objections set out above. Membership of the management boards would presumably be highly attractive to councillors because of its functions and status; the addition of the salary will serve to augment the distinction between the management board and 'backbench' councillors. It will add to the tensions involved in selecting the management board. Another aspect is how far the public will understand that not all councillors are paid. The backbench councillor may be irked by his limited functions under the Maud scheme; he will be even more irritated should it be generally believed that he is getting a salary. Even if it is widely appreciated that only the management boards are paid and it is widely known who are the members of the local board, anyone standing at a council election will appear to be hoping for a salary. In fact, many people will stand without any hope or perhaps intention of receiving one. And many councillors will have little chance of reaching the management board, either for political reasons, lack of experience or personal unpopularity with their fellow councillors.

One must not paint too gloomy a picture. If payment is introduced some development of mistrust is inevitable. As the new conditions of local government work become established and accepted, much of the mistrust will die away. A social democracy that is moving away from extremes of wealth and poverty has no leisured independent group of citizens able to undertake all public duties – even supposing it is desirable that all public offices be filled by a limited elite. The central justification for payment is not that it will produce better councillors, but that it is only fair to councillors that they should, if they wish, receive some recompense. One other advantage is that the institution of salaries would enhance the prospect of abolishing aldermen, for there would be democratic objection to paying those who hold office by indirect election.

The future geographical pattern of local authorities also affects the question of payment. If there are a small number of regional size top-tier authorities each comprising a small number of councillors, so that every councillor represents an area not dissimilar in size to a parliamentary constituency, then there would be little difficulty about paying salaries to all members of regional authorities. But if there are to be thirty or forty top-tier authorities each with up to, say, seventy-five elected members and operating through a Maud-style management board – or something similar – then it is likely that payments will be limited to the inner or managing group of councillors. The question of whether any salaries would be paid to councillors in second-tier authorities might again depend on the size of these authorities. It is notable that the Maud Committee did not mention any minimum size of authority below which salaries should not be paid; presumably they assumed that a drastic slaughter of the small and medium-size councils would be made.

Thus the questions of payment, the size of authorities, the functions of councillors and methods of administration are inseparable. If our local government is to be efficient, is to move away from the cult of the amateur, is to be capable of responding to contemporary needs – then major reforms are required. This does not mean that all the ideas presented by Lord Redcliffe-Maud to the nation for consideration will, or should be, adopted. It does mean that British local government should be prepared for perhaps the biggest overhaul it has ever undergone to produce a new local government system.

*Appendices*

## APPENDIX A. DISTRIBUTION OF FUNCTIONS

The following lists show the distribution between the several classes of local authority of local government services and functions in alphabetical order. They are subject to some local variations, *e.g.* Local Act Powers; some powers are mandatory and others permissive. As between councils of the same class, there are some differences in the powers and duties, dependent on the population of the district or the extent to which powers have been delegated by the County Council or conferred by the Minister of Housing and Local Government or exercised by joint boards or joint committees constituted from local authorities.

| Powers and Duties of Local Authorities | County Councils | County Borough Councils | Non-County Borough Councils | Urban District Councils | Rural District Councils | Parish Councils (Rural) | Greater London Council | London Borough Councils |
|---|---|---|---|---|---|---|---|---|
| Abattoirs – provision and maintenance | — | Yes | Yes | Yes | Yes | — | — | Yes |
| Access to the Countryside | Yes | Yes | (Yes) | (Yes) (where delegated) | (Yes) | — | — | Yes |
| Administration of Justice | Yes | Yes | Some | — | — | — | Yes | — |
| Aerodromes, provision of | Yes | Yes | Yes | Yes | Yes | — | Yes | Yes |
| Aged and Infirm, accommodation and welfare | Yes | Yes | — | — | — | — | — | Yes |
| Agricultural Education | Yes | Yes | — | — | — | — | Yes | Yes |
| Allotments and Smallholdings | Yes | Yes | Allotments only | Allotments only | Allotments only | Allotments only | Inner London Smallholdings only | Outer London Allotments only |
| Alteration of areas of county districts | Yes | — | — | — | — | — | — | — |
| Ambulances | Yes | Yes | — | — | — | — | Yes | — |

| Powers and Duties of Local Authorities | County Councils | County Borough Councils | Non-County Borough Councils | Urban District Councils | Rural District Councils | Parish Councils (Rural) | Greater London Council | London Borough Councils |
|---|---|---|---|---|---|---|---|---|
| Approved schools | Yes | Yes | — | — | — | — | Yes | — |
| Art Galleries – construction and supervision | Yes | Yes | Yes | Yes | Yes | Yes | Yes | Yes |
| Baths, swimming baths, wash-houses and laundries | — | Yes | Yes | Yes | Yes | Yes | — | Yes |
| Betting and Gaming Act, 1960. (Permits for provision of Amusements with prizes) | — | Yes | Yes | Yes | Yes | — | — | Yes |
| Births, deaths and marriages registration | Yes | Yes | — | — | — | — | — | Yes |
| Blind, deaf, dumb and crippled – welfare | Yes | Yes | — | — | — | — | — | Yes |
| Bridges – construction and maintenance | Yes | Yes | — | — | — | — | Yes | Yes |
| Bridges – lighting | — | Yes | Yes | Yes | Yes | — | — | Yes |
| Building control | — | Yes | Yes | Yes | Yes | — | Yes | Yes |
| Building preservation | Yes | Yes | Yes | Yes | Yes | — | Yes (Inner London) | Yes (Outer London) |
| Burial grounds, cemeteries, crematoria and mortuaries | Crematoria only | Yes | Yes | Yes | Yes (except burial grounds) | Burial grounds and mortuaries only | — | Yes |
| Byelaws, various | Yes | Yes | Yes | Yes | Yes | Yes | Yes | Yes |

| | | | | | | | |
|---|---|---|---|---|---|---|---|
| Canal boats – registration and inspection | — | Yes | — | Yes | Yes | — | Yes |
| Caravans, site licences | — | Yes | — | Yes | Yes | — | — |
| Caravans, provision of sites | Yes | Yes | Yes | Yes | Yes | Yes | Yes |
| Cattle grids | Yes | Yes | Yes | Yes | Yes | Yes | Yes |
| Celluloid – storage control | — | Yes | Yes | Yes | — | — | Yes |
| Charities Act, 1960 (various powers) | Yes | Yes | Yes | Yes | Yes | Yes | Yes |
| Children – adoption, boarding out, control of employment, protection | Yes | Yes | Yes | Yes | Yes | Yes | Yes |
| Civic Restaurants | Yes | Yes | — | Yes | — | — | Yes |
| Civil Defence | — | Yes | Yes | Yes | — | Yes | Yes |
| Clean Air Act – Smoke Abatement | — | Yes | (minor responsibilities & powers) | — | — | Yes | Yes |
| Clocks | Yes | Yes | Yes | Yes | Yes | Yes | Yes |
| Coast Protection | Yes | Yes | Yes | Yes | Yes | — | Yes |
| Common Lodging Houses | — | Yes | Yes | Yes | Yes | — | — |
| Commons | Yes | Yes | Yes | Yes | Yes | Yes | Yes |
| Community Centres | Yes | Yes | Yes | Yes | Yes | Yes | Yes |
| Consumer Protection Act, 1961 | Yes | Yes | Yes | Yes | Yes | — | Yes |
| Coroners | Yes | Yes | — | — | — | Yes | — |
| Day Nurseries | Yes | Yes | — | — | — | — | Yes |
| Diseases of animals, sterilisation of waste food, foot and mouth disease | Yes | Yes | — | — | — | — | Yes |

| Powers and Duties of Local Authorities | County Councils | County Borough Councils | Non-County Borough Councils | Urban District Councils | Rural District Councils | Parish Councils (Rural) | Greater London Council | London Borough Councils |
|---|---|---|---|---|---|---|---|---|
| Elections | Yes | Yes | Yes | Yes | Yes | Yes | Yes | Yes |
| Education, including school medical service school meals road patrols | Yes | Yes | (Yes) (where delegated or conferred under various arrangements) | (Yes) | (Yes) | — | Yes Inner London | Yes Outer London |
| Entertainment – licensing of theatres, cinemas, race courses, music and dancing establishments, boxing and wrestling arenas | Yes | Yes | — | — | — | — | Yes | — |
| Entertainment – provision of | — | Yes | Yes | Yes | Yes | — | Yes | Yes |
| Explosives and fireworks | Yes | Yes | Yes | Yes | Yes | — | Yes | Yes |
| Factories – health and sanitary conditions | — | Yes | Yes | Yes | Yes | — | — | Yes |
| Fertilizers and feeding-stuffs – analysis | Yes | Yes | — | — | — | — | — | Yes |
| Fireguards inspection | — | Yes | Yes | Yes | Yes | — | — | Yes |
| Fire services | Yes | Yes | — | — | — | — | Yes | — |
| Food and Drugs – inspection, sampling and analysis | Yes | Yes | Yes | Yes | Yes | — | — | Yes |

| | | | | | | | |
|---|---|---|---|---|---|---|---|
| Footpaths – repair and maintenance, long distance routes, survey, diversion and closure | Yes | Yes | Yes | Yes | Yes (not long distance routes) | Yes | Yes |
| **HEALTH SERVICES:** Local Health Services: | | | | | | | |
| (i) Maternity and Child Welfare | Yes | Yes | (Yes) | (Yes) (where delegated) | — | — | Yes |
| (ii) Midwives | | | | | | | |
| (iii) Health visitors | | | | | | | |
| (iv) Domestic helps | | | | | | | |
| (v) Health centres | | | | | | | |
| (vi) Vaccination and immunisation | | | | | | | |
| (vii) Home Nursing | | | | | | | |
| (viii) Prevention of illness | | | | | | | |
| (ix) Care and after-care of sick | | | | | | | |
| (x) Mental Health | | | | | | | |
| Housing, including provision of houses, slum clearance, re-development, over-crowding, improvement grants | — | Yes | Yes | Yes | — | Yes (out-county housing) | Yes |
| Lodging temporarily homeless people | Yes | Yes | — | — | — | — | Yes |
| Housing conditions – supervision in rural areas | Yes | — | — | — | — | — | — |
| Housing for employees, provision | Yes | — | — | — | — | — | — |

| Powers and Duties of Local Authorities | County Councils | County Borough Councils | Non-County Borough Councils | Urban District Councils | Rural District Councils | Parish Councils (Rural) | Greater London Council | London Borough Councils |
|---|---|---|---|---|---|---|---|---|
| Housing mortgage advances (under Housing Acts or Small Dwellings Acquisition Acts) and including giving guarantee to Building Societies | Yes | Yes | Yes | Yes | Yes | — | — | Yes |
| Infectious diseases — notification, disinfection and prevention | — | Yes | Yes | Yes | Yes | — | — | Yes |
| Information centres | Yes | Yes | Yes | Yes | Yes | — | Yes | Yes |
| Land Acquisition | Yes | Yes | Yes | Yes | Yes | — | Yes | Yes |
| Land charges registration | Yes | Yes | Yes | Yes | Yes | — | — | Yes |
| Land drainage | Yes | Yes | — | — | — | — | Yes | Yes |
| Legal Aid (Legal Aid and Advice Act, 1949) | Yes | — | — | — | — | — | — | — |
| Libraries and museums | Yes | Yes | Some | Some | Museums only | Some Libraries only | Yes Museums only | Yes |
| Licences – dogs, game, guns, hackney carriages and drivers, hawkers, money-lenders, nurses' agencies, | | | | | | | | |

| | | | | | | Naming of streets | Numbering of houses |
|---|---|---|---|---|---|---|---|
| pawnbrokers, pet animals, petroleum, milk, slaughterhouses, rag flock, poisons, masseur, hairdressing, employment agencies | Various | Various | Various | Various | Various | — | Yes |
| Life-saving apparatus | Yes | Yes | Yes | Yes | — | — | — |
| Litter Act | Yes | Yes | Yes | Yes | Yes | Yes | Yes |
| Markets | Yes | Yes | Yes | Yes (with consent of Minister) | — | — | Yes |
| Meat inspection at slaughterhouses | Yes | Yes | Yes | Yes | — | — | Yes |
| Milk inspection | Yes | Yes | Yes | Yes | — | — | Yes |
| Motor vehicles and drivers' licensing | Yes | — | — | — | — | Yes | — |
| Naming of streets and numbering of houses | — | Yes | Yes | Yes | — | | |
| National Assistance Act: welfare functions | Yes | Yes | Yes (where delegated) | Yes | — | — | Yes |
| National Parks – establishment of nature reserves | Yes | (county districts can act with the consent of the county council and the Nature Conservancy) | | | — | — | — |
| National Parks and Areas of outstanding Natural Beauty | Yes | Yes | — | — | — | — | Yes |
| Nuisances – suppression of | — | Yes | Yes | Yes | Yes | Yes | Yes |

| Powers and Duties of Local Authorities | County Councils | County Borough Councils | Non-County Borough Councils | Urban District Councils | Rural District Councils | Parish Councils (Rural) | Greater London Council | London Borough Councils |
|---|---|---|---|---|---|---|---|---|
| Nurseries and child minders regulation | Yes | Yes | Yes | Yes | Yes | — | — | Yes |
| Nursing Homes registration | Yes | Yes | — | — | — | — | — | Yes |
| Offensive trades – authorisation and inspection | — | Yes | Yes | Yes | Yes | — | — | Yes |
| Offices Act, 1960: Enforcement by L.As. of regulations made by Home Secretary | — | Yes | Yes | Yes | Yes | — | — | Yes |
| Oil Burners Act, 1960 – enforcement by L.As. of regulations made by Home Secretary | — | Yes | Yes | Yes | Yes | — | — | Yes |
| Omnibus shelters | Yes | Yes | Yes | Yes | Yes | Yes | Yes | Yes |
| Parking Places | Yes (In a National Park or area of outstanding natural beauty) | Yes | Yes | Yes | Yes | — | Yes | Yes |

| Function | | | | | | |
|---|---|---|---|---|---|---|
| Parks, Open Spaces, pleasure and recreation grounds | Yes | Yes | Yes | Yes | Yes | Yes |
| Physical Training and Recreation Act, 1937, for the provision of gymnasia, camping sites, etc. | Yes | Yes (Cambridge and Peterborough) | Yes | Yes | Yes | Yes |
| Police (outside Metropolitan Police area) | Yes | — | — | — | — | — |
| Pool Betting Act, 1954 – Registration of pools promoters | Yes | — | — | — | Yes | — |
| Port Health, including action under Aliens Orders, 1920–1953 | Yes | Yes | Yes | Yes | Yes | — |
| Prevention of damage by pests, including rodent control | Yes | Yes | Yes | Yes | — | Yes |
| Private Street Works | Yes (in rural areas) | Yes | Yes | Yes | — | Yes |
| Protection of Animals, performing pets | Yes / Yes / Some | — / Yes / — | — / Yes / — | — / Yes / — | — / Yes / — | — / Yes / — |
| Probation Service | Yes | Yes | Yes | Yes | — | — |
| Public Conveniences | Yes | Yes | Yes | Yes | — | Yes |
| Public Transport | — | Yes | Yes | — | — | Yes |
| Rates – levying and collection | — | Yes | Yes | Yes | — | Yes |

| Powers and Duties of Local Authorities | County Councils | County Borough Councils | Non-County Borough Councils | Urban District Councils | Rural District Councils | Parish Councils (Rural) | Greater London Council | London Borough Councils |
|---|---|---|---|---|---|---|---|---|
| Refuse collection and disposal | — | Yes | Yes | Yes | Yes | — | Disposal only | Yes |
| Registration of electors | — | Yes | Yes | Yes | Yes | — | — | Yes |
| Remand Homes | Yes | Yes | — | — | — | — | Yes | — |
| Rent Control (various powers) | — | Yes | Yes | Yes | Yes | — | — | Yes |
| Reservoirs – safety of | Yes | Yes | Yes | Yes | Yes | — | — | Yes |
| River Boards, representation on | Yes | Yes | — | — | — | — | — | — |
| Road safety | — | Yes | Yes | Yes | Yes | — | — | Yes |
| Roads: (i) construction | Yes | Yes | — | — | — | — | Yes | Yes |
| (ii) maintenance | Yes | Yes | Yes | Yes | — | — | Yes | Yes |
| (iii) lighting | — | Yes | Yes | Yes | Yes | Yes | Yes | Yes |
| Sanitary (Public Health) services | — | Yes | Yes | Yes | Yes | — | — | Yes |
| Sea Fisheries Act | Yes | Yes | — | — | — | — | — | — |
| Sewerage and Sewage disposal | — | Yes | Yes | Yes | Yes | — | Yes | Yes |
| Shops Inspection | Yes | Yes | Yes | Yes | Yes | — | Yes | Yes |
| Small Lotteries and Gaming Act, 1956 | — | Yes | Yes | Yes | Yes | — | — | Yes |
| Town and Country Planning: 1. Preparation and revision of development plan | Yes | Yes | — | — | — | — | Yes | — |

| | | | | | | |
|---|---|---|---|---|---|---|
| 2. Planning control, including advertisement control and the preservation of trees | Yes | (Yes) (where delegated) | (Yes) | — | — | Yes |
| Town Development Act, 1952 (powers vary as to whether receiving or disposing of population) | Yes | Yes | Yes | — | Yes | Yes |
| Town Halls, Council Offices, Parish Halls, etc. | Yes | Yes | Yes | Yes | Yes | Yes |
| Vaccination and immunisation | Yes | — | — | — | — | Yes |
| Valuation, miscellaneous powers | Yes | Yes | Yes | — | Yes | Yes |
| War Memorials – maintenance | Yes | Yes | Yes | Yes | — | Yes |
| Water courses – sanitary control of | — Anglesey only | Yes | Yes | Yes | Yes | Yes |
| Water Supply | Yes | Yes | Yes | — | — | — |
| Weights and Measures – inspection | Yes (if popn. 10,000 or over) | — | — | — | — | Yes |
| Welfare services for aged and handicapped | Yes | — | — | — | — | Yes |
| Wild Birds Protection Act | Yes | Yes | Yes | — | Yes | Yes |

| Powers and Duties of Local Authorities | County Councils | County Borough Councils | Non-County Borough Councils | Urban District Councils | Rural District Councils | Parish Councils (Rural) | Greater London Council | London Borough Councils |
|---|---|---|---|---|---|---|---|---|
| Youth Employment Service (except where service is operated by Ministry of Labour and National Service) | Yes | Yes | — | — | — | — | Yes Inner London | Yes Outer London |

**NOTES:**

The Common Council of the City of London has similar but not identical, functions to the London Boroughs.

'Inner London' refers to the area of the old L.C.C.

'Outer London' refers to that part of the Greater London area outside the old L.C.C.

This table is based on material supplied by the Ministry of Housing and Local Government. I am most grateful to the Ministry for their assistance.

## APPENDIX B. LOCAL AUTHORITY POPULATIONS

The table below gives a broad picture of the variations in size of local authorities. It is based on information in the *Municipal Year Book, 1967.*

| Population 000s | County Councils | County Boroughs | Non-County Boroughs | Urban Districts | Rural Districts | Rural Boroughs | London Boroughs |
|---|---|---|---|---|---|---|---|
| Over 1000 | 5 | 1 | — | — | — | — | — |
| 500–1000 | 13 | 3 | — | — | — | — | — |
| 400–500 | 9 | 2 | — | — | — | — | — |
| 300–400 | 6 | 2 | — | — | — | — | 7 |
| 200–300 | 6 | 10 | — | — | — | — | 20 |
| 100–200 | 9 | 33 | — | 2 | — | — | 5 |
| 90–100 | 2 | 2 | 4 | 1 | 2 | — | — |
| 80–90 | — | 7 | 3 | 1 | 1 | — | — |
| 70–80 | 1 | 10 | 10 | 2 | 2 | — | — |
| 60–70 | 3 | 6 | 8 | 5 | 11 | — | — |
| 50–60 | 1 | 5 | 21 | 7 | 15 | — | — |
| 40–50 | 1 | 1 | 27 | 15 | 22 | — | — |
| 30–40 | 1 | — | 32 | 35 | 48 | — | — |
| 20–30 | 1 | — | 32 | 77 | 94 | — | — |
| 15–20 | — | — | 26 | 77 | 76 | — | — |
| 10–15 | — | — | 24 | 83 | 82 | 1 | — |
| 5–10 | — | — | 35 | 128 | 82 | 3 | — |
| Under 5 | — | — | 43 | 102 | 37 | 2 | — |
| TOTALS | 58 | 82 | 265 | 535 | 472 | 6 | 32 |

The Greater London Council and the City of London are excluded from the table.

## REPRESENTATION ON OUTSIDE BODIES:
### THE ASSOCIATION OF MUNICIPAL CORPORATIONS

Aircraft Control Advisory Committee, Civil
Airports Committee of Local Authorities, Joint (J.A.C.O.L.A.)
Allotments Advisory Committee
Birds, Advisory Committee on the Protection of (England and Wales)
Blind, Royal National Institute for the
Blind, Ltd, Industrial Advisers to the
Blind Persons, Ministry of Labour Committee on Training and Employment of
Blind Workers, Local Authorities' Advisory Committee on Conditions of Service of
Bridges Over Railways, Maintenance of – Working Party
Cinema Consultative Committee
Coal Consumers' Council, Domestic
Composting, Municipal Joint Working Party
Computer Committee, Local Government
Conditions of Service Advisory Board, Local Authorities'
Contracts Tribunal (RIBA), Joint
Dangerous Substances, Standing Advisory Committee on
Deaf, Royal National Institute for the
Development Control, Management Study of
District Nursing, Queen's Institute of
Education, Advisory Committee on Adult (Independent Television Authority)
Education, N.A.C. for Art
Education, National Committee for Audio-Visual Aids in
Education, National Co-operating Body for (UNESCO)
Education (England and Wales), National Institute of Adult
Education Advisory Committee (Associated Television, Ltd)
Education Advisory Council, Further (BBC)
Education Board, Public Health Inspectors'
Education in World Citizenship, Council for (United Nations Association)
Educational Advisory Committee (Associated Rediffusion Ltd)
Educational Foundation for Visual Aids
Educational Interchange Council
Educational Research, National Foundation for
Epilepsy Association, British
Examination Board, City and Guilds of London Institute
Examinations Board, Local Government
Examinations, Oxford Delegacy of Local
Examinations Syndicate, University of Cambridge Local
Examining Board, Associated
Family Planning Association
Field Studies Council
Films for Children, National Centre of

Fire Brigades Advisory Council, Central
Fire Service Building Projects (Working Party)
Fire Service College – Board of Management
Fire Services Central Examinations Board
Food Production, National Council for Domestic
Food Standards, Local Authorities' Joint Advisory Committee on
Handicapped, Advisory Committee for the Health and Welfare of the
    (Ministry of Health)
Health Education, Central Council for
Health Services Council, Central
Health Visitors' Training Council
Historic Towns and Cities Conference Project
House Workers, National Institute of – Advisory Council
Hygiene and Tropical Medicine, London School of (Court of Governors)
Industry, Confederation of British – Joint Fire Panel of the Production
    Committee
Information Service, Local Government – Management Committee
Inter-Authority Payments, Local Education Authorities' Advisory Com-
    mittee on
International Union of Local Authorities (British Section)
'Keep Britain Tidy Group' (Council)
Local Government Studies, Institute of (University of Birmingham) –
    Steering Committee
Local Authorities' Mutual Investment Trust (LAMIT)
Mental Health, National Association for – Advisory Council
Merchant Navy Training Board
Midwives Board, Central
Motor Rallies Advisory Committee
Museums, British National Committee of the International Council of
Museums and Galleries, Standing Commission on
Nursery Examination Board, National
Nurses and Midwives, National Consultative Council on the Recruit-
    ment of
Oil Pollution of the Sea, Advisory Committee on
Old People's Welfare Council, National
Physical Recreation, Central Council of
Playing Fields Association, National – Council
Police Advisory Board
Police College, Board of Governors
Police Promotion Examinations Board
Police Services, Central Committee on Common
Police Training Committee, Higher
Post Office Users' Council
Public Administration, Royal Institute of
Public Utilities Street Works Act, 1950 – Working Party
Rating and Valuation Working Party (Nationalized Industries)
Records Association, British – Records Preservation Section
Savings Committee, National – Local Authorities' Advisory Committee
School Broadcasting Council for United Kingdom (BBC)
Schoolchildren, Council for Colony Holidays for
Schools Broadcast Advisory Committee (Granada Television Network)
Schools Council for Curriculum and Examinations
Site Services, Committee on Co-ordination of

Smoking and Health – Health Education Co-ordinating Committee
Social Service, National Council of
Social Work Advisory Service
Social Work Training, National Institute for
Social Workers Training Council
Spastics Society
Staff College, Administrative – L.A.s Joint Admissions Committee
Staff College, Further Education (Board of Governors)
Standards Institution, British
Superannuation Scheme for Nurses and Hospital Officers, Federated –
  Council and Executive
Sutton Dwellings Trust
Teachers of the Mentally Handicapped, Training Council for
Teachers Overseas, National Advisory Council for the Supply of
Theatre, Standing Advisory Committee on Local Authorities and the,
  (SACLAT)
Trade Effluent Joint Advisory Panel (TEJAP)
Training Board, Local Government
Travel Association, British
'Twinning' Committee, Joint
University Awards: Joint Committee of Local Authority Associations
  and Vice-Chancellors and Principals
Waste Paper Co-ordinating Committee
Water Pollution Research, United Kingdom Committee on
Youth Employment Council
Youth Employment Service Training Board

### NEGOTIATING BODIES

Administrative, Professional, Technical and Clerical Services, N.J.C. for
  Local Authorities'
Approved Schools and Remand Homes, J.N.C. for
Blind, N.J.C. for Workshops for the
Building and Civil Engineering, J.N.C. for
Burnham Committees
Chief Officers of Local Authorities, J.N.C. for
Engineering Craftsmen, J.N.C. for
Fire Brigades, N.J.C. for
Fire Officers, N.J.C. for Chief
Health Services (Great Britain), Whitley Councils for the
Justices' Clerks, J.N.C. for
Justices' Clerks' Assistants, J.N.C. for
Manual Workers, N.J.C. for Local Authorities' Services
Places of Refreshment Wages Board, Unlicensed
Police Council for Great Britain
Probation Service in England and Wales, J.N.C. for the
Towns Clerks and District Council Clerks, J.N.C. for
Water Engineers' Salaries, J.C. for
Youth Leaders and Community Centre Wardens, J.N.C. for

Source: *Annual Report of the A.M.C. 1967*

# INDEX